STUDY GUIDE
FOR
ENTRIES & EXITS

Founded in 1807, John Wiley & Sons is the oldest independent publishing company in the United States. With offices in North America, Europe, Australia, and Asia, Wiley is globally committed to developing and marketing print and electronic products and services for our customers' professional and personal knowledge and understanding.

The Wiley Trading series features books by traders who have survived the market's ever-changing temperament and have prospered—some by reinventing systems, others by getting back to basics. Whether a novice trader, professional, or somewhere in-between, these books will provide the advice and strategies needed to prosper today and well into the future.

For a list of available titles, please visit our Web site at www.WileyFinance.com.

STUDY GUIDE
FOR
ENTRIES & EXITS

VISITS TO SIXTEEN TRADING ROOMS

DR. ALEXANDER ELDER

WILEY

John Wiley & Sons, Inc.

CONTENTS

Study Guide
for
Entries & Exits

HOW THIS BOOK IS ORGANIZED

Creating this *Study Guide* was a challenge. The publisher wanted to build on the success of my previous study guides. Creating them for *Trading for a Living* and *Come into My Trading Room* had been quite straightforward because both main books were completely mine; I knew them by heart. All I had to do was ask questions about my own text to cover all the bases.

Entries & Exits, by contrast, reflects the methods of 16 traders. They were kind enough to open their trading rooms, show me their trades, and spend hours answering questions. I could not burden them any further by asking them to write test questions—it would have been too much. But the publisher wanted a *Study Guide*, and I did not want to let her down.

Since you have probably already read *Entries & Exits*, you know that certain key themes came up again and again in many interviews: psychology, discipline, risk control, planning, and a handful of chart patterns and technical indicators. I decided to make this *Study Guide* different from my previous ones. Instead of linking each question to a specific interview, I decided to link all questions to the major areas of trading.

There are seven chapters in both the Questions and the Answers sections of this *Study Guide*. We start with Organization, Psychology, Markets, Trading Tactics, and Money Management and Record-Keeping. Then we will go into Case Studies and real-life trading examples. In the final section, Traders Speak, I'll quiz you about some of the key points raised by traders in their interviews. All questions should encourage you to dig deeper into *Entries & Exits* and think about the essentials of the decision-making process.

Each year I have several happy encounters when I run into traders who shake my hand and tell me that they had moved up to trading for a living after they read my books or studied with me. I created this *Study Guide* to help you focus on your work, and I would like nothing better than to know that it helped you discover how to trade for a living.

I wish you success.

QUESTIONS

ORGANIZATION

When a surgeon walks into his operating room, he knows that all the equipment has been set up to help him achieve success. The life-support instruments, the surgical supplies, and the systems for dealing with emergencies are all in place before he begins. Similarly, when you begin trading, you have to prepare your trading room before placing orders. You must choose your software and learn to use it, and you must allocate capital, money, and time. You need to develop a plan of action and emergency procedures, taking care of a host of important details.

This section will help you review what you need to do to prepare yourself to trade. A mere dozen questions cannot cover every step and procedure, but they can serve as a wake-up call. If you do well, you are more likely to succeed, but if you do poorly on these tests, you should stop and do some serious studying before putting a dollar at risk.

Questions	Max. Pts. Available	Trial 1	Trial 2	Trial 3	Trial 4
1	1				
2	1				
3	1				
4	1				
5	1				
6	1				
7	1				
8	1				
9	1				
10	1				
11	1				
12	1				
13	1				
Total points	13				

Question 1—Learning to Trade

How long should it take to become a successful trader?

A. As long as it takes to learn to drive a car

B. Double the length of time it takes to read ten trading books and master two software packages

C. As long as it takes to get a college education

D. It depends on the amount of time you can invest on a regular basis

Question 2—A Very Small Account

Starting to trade with a very small account presents several unique challenges. Trading-related expenses consume a larger percentage, and the margin of safety is reduced. Which two of the following recommendations are essential?

A. Stay away from the market until you can fund a bigger amount.

B. Trade aggressively to make a difference; suspend the 2% Rule.

C. Find a broker who will allow you to trade 100 shares for $1 commission.

D. Trade options instead of stocks.

E. Do not try to make a lot of money but build a steady track record.

Question 3—Time Management

Seeing how a trader manages time can tell you a great deal about his seriousness or lack of such. Please review the following descriptions and identify which apply to a professional trader, a serious amateur, or a gambler:

A. Attaches an alarm to a five-minute chart to remind himself to look at the market every five minutes and not miss any signals

B. Spends three hours reviewing the markets every weekend, half an hour every evening

C. Makes notes of companies in the news and looks up their stocks in his charting program

D. Avoids looking at his computer on the days when his positions are underwater

E. Spends several hours each day in front of the screen and does not allow himself to have dinner before updating that day's entries and exits

Question 4—Paper-Trading

Paper-trading is to real trading what photo-hunting is to hunting with a rifle. You have to go into the wilderness and find your prey, only instead of shooting, you make a photographic record of it. Which of the following features make paper-trading a useful activity?

A. It tests your ability to perform daily homework and track positions.

B. It allows you to test new trading ideas without risking money.

C. It prepares you for placing orders, including stops.

D. It shows you exactly what to expect in real-money trading.

Choose the correct answer:

1. None of the above

2. A

3. A and B

4. A, B, and C

5. All are correct

Question 5—Choosing Hardware

Please select a configuration of hardware that can be used for trading for a living:

A. A single laptop

B. A fast computer with dual screens

C. Two computers

D. Two computers with dual screens, plus a mobile quote device

Choose the correct answer:

1. A

2. A and B

3. A, B, and C

4. All are correct

Question 6—Choosing Software

A professional trader can base his trading decisions on any single tool among the following, except for which two?

A. Manual charting

B. A free chart Web site with 20-minute delayed data

C. A daily advisory with charts and specific recommendations

D. A toolbox package with real-time datafeed

E. A blackbox package delivering specific trading signals

Question 7—Using Excel

Many traders use Excel to maintain records and organize homework. Some perform extensive programming, while others do not use spreadsheets at all. Knowing which Excel functions is useful for serious traders?

A. Designing a basic spreadsheet to hold data and perform automatic calculations across data columns

B. Using formulas, including absolute and relative references

C. Using conditional formatting and the Chart Wizard

D. Knowing how to write Visual Basic code

Choose the correct answer:

1. None of the above

2. A

3. A and B

4. A, B, and C

5. All of the above

Question 8—A Black Box

A broker invites you to open an S&P trading account with his firm. He suggests you purchase a commercially available automatic system, and he will trade its signals for you. Which course of action makes sense?

A. Make sure the system has been backtested.

B. Ask to diversify into other markets, in addition to the S&P.

C. Ask for reduced commissions.

D. Ask for the system's performance record.

E. Hang up on the broker.

Question 9—Allocating Time

After a year of part-time trading, a person reorganizes his business life to free up one day per week. Trading has become a serious hobby for him, and he decides to invest more time in it. Please review the following choices: Each line offers two, and you need to decide whether A (the first option) or B (the second option) is preferable.

1. Add group analysis to your study of the stock market or diversify into futures?

2. Develop more elaborate records or add two additional timeframes to weekly and daily charts?

3. Learn to use a more advanced charting package or become more proficient in Excel?

4. Dedicate your free day to day-trading or use it to backtest your system on a greater number of markets?

Question 10—Allocating money

A beginning trader with $50,000 in his account learns about controlling expenses and decides to allocate $2,000 a year to education. Please review the following choices: Each line offers two, and you need to decide whether A (the first option) or B (the second option) is preferable.

1. Buy a $250 software package or a $1,200 advanced version of that software?

2. Spend $30 a month on data or look for free data on the Internet?

3. Spend $300 on books or $1,000 on private tutoring?

4. Spend $500 to subscribe to an advisory service or to attend a conference?

Question 11—Networking with Traders

Some ways of networking with other traders can help you, while others can derail you. Which two of the following activities are likely to be useful?

A. Have a trading buddy with whom you can review completed trades.

B. Have a circle of friends who can vote on going long or short.

C. Join as many Internet forums as possible.

D. Make sure to contribute to a forum or a group on a regular basis.

Question 12—Creating a Trading Checklist

Aircraft pilots go through a preflight checklist to make sure their plane is ready for takeoff. Some serious traders follow their example and prepare a checklist. They apply it to every trade before placing an order. Please review the following statements and identify three correct ones:

A. Even an incomplete checklist is better than no checklist at all.

B. The more rules in the checklist, the more reliable it is.

C. A checklist must ensure compliance with money management rules.

D. A checklist must identify the source of the trade.

E. A checklist must review the broad market.

Question 13—Organizing for a Better Outcome

Traders need to make many decisions on how to organize their trading. Some of these choices will have a greater impact on your outcome than even market analysis. Please review the following choices: Each line offers two, and you need to decide whether A (the first option) or B (the second option) is preferable.

1. Finding a stock to buy or planning an exit?

2. Risking $100 in an attempt to make $200 or risking $500 in an attempt to make $1,250?

3. Focus on the outcome of the current trade or that of an average trade?

4. Have six open trades, each risking 1% or three trades, each risking 2%?

PSYCHOLOGY

Your feelings, hopes, and fears have a major impact on your performance. How you process market information is just as important as the information itself. This huge importance of your personality is something that new traders tend to miss. They pay the price for this oversight in repeated losses, until they either wake up or wash out of the markets.

Questions in this section are designed to alert you to several aspects of trading psychology. As you answer them, keep in mind that there are many subtle and not so subtle differences in the feelings and thinking of various people. There is no single mindset you have to fit. What you need is to find out how you think and feel and then decide what types of trading are best suited to your personality.

Questions	Max. Pts. Available	Trial 1	Trial 2	Trial 3	Trial 4
14	1				
15	1				
16	1				
17	1				
18	1				
19	1				
20	1				
21	1				
22	1				
23	1				
24	1				
25	1				
26	1				
Total points	13				

Question 14—Trader's Development

A trader needs to acquire a body of knowledge and make sure his psychology is in gear with the markets. Please review the following five statements and indicate which three are correct:

A. Having specific targets close to the markets is useful for beginning traders even though potential profits are reduced.

B. Taking courses on the Internet can help improve one's trading performance.

C. Making many small trades helps raise the confidence level.

D. Successful trading has nothing to do with one's philosophy of life.

E. A trader's performance tends to change over time in one steady trend—winners keep getting better and losers keep going down.

Question 15—Self-Imposed Limits

A private trader does not have to report to anyone how he performs, and this lack of accountability creates many temptations to misbehave and cut corners. A serious trader who wishes to avoid the temptations of irresponsible trading creates rules that place limits on his activities. All of the following limits are essential, except for which one?

A. Set up and strictly observe money management rules.

B. Do not allow a profit greater than some minimal number to turn into a loss.

C. Diversify your account into a specific number of positions.

D. Do not add to losing positions, unless planned in advance as a part of building a large position.

E. Use protective stops.

Question 16—A Scientific Background

A person with a scientific background has advantages and disadvantages in trading. Please identify which statements on the list below are advantages and which are disadvantages:

A. A habit for working with numbers

B. Expecting to reach a state of certainty through good research

C. A willingness to hold a losing trade if the entry was based on solid rules

D. Valuing technical studies above trading psychology

E. Having an ingrained habit of keeping records

Question 17—Activity Level

Traders tend to be energetic people whose activity level is expressed by how frequently they trade. Which two of the following statements about their activity are correct?

A. The more trades you put on, the faster you can learn.

B. You must set a maximum number of trades per week and not exceed that level.

C. There are always enough opportunities in the market; if you see no trade, change your system.

D. It is more important to study the market every day than to trade every day.

E. Anything that slows down trading, such as extensive note-keeping, should be eliminated.

Question 18—Uncertainty in the Markets

Buy and sell signals are clearly visible in the middle of the chart but become increasingly foggy near the right edge. This lack of clarity frustrates beginners, but the ability to deal with uncertainty is a hall-mark of professional trading. Which two of the following five statements about uncertainty are true?

A. Wait for indicator signals to be confirmed by price action, such as breaking of a trendline, support, or resistance before entering a trade.

B. A trade following a relatively foggy signal with a tight stop is preferable to a trade with a clear signal and a wide stop.

C. You should wait for all indicators to be in gear before putting on a trade.

D. When the markets are especially uncertain, it is a good time to review public media to find the consensus about an emerging trend.

E. Certainty is an unreachable goal; the search for certainty hurts traders, especially those who come from scientific backgrounds.

Question 19—Asking for Advice

An experienced trader finds several e-mails in his inbox. A quick glance helps him decide which one merits a reply:

A. A stranger asks where to find free data on the Internet

B. A beginner asks what trading methods to use to provide for his family

C. A trader asks about recommended indicator settings

D. A trader asks you to take a look at a new method he invented

E. A trader asks for a list of mentors in his area

Question 20—Sharing Information

As you study the markets, it may feel natural to share your findings with others, use their tips, and reciprocate with your own. Which three of the following statements regarding such sharing are true?

A. When a trusted friend tells you about his position, it is a good idea to duplicate it.

B. It is a good idea to discuss planned trades with friends.

C. It is nice to let your friends know which trades you are in.

D. It is a good idea to discuss your completed trades with friends.

E. A tip should be put into your trading system to test whether your rules confirm it.

F. It is important to write down which person gave you which tip.

Question 21—Gaming and Trading

There are many similarities and differences between trading and games that combine skill and chance, such as blackjack or betting on horses. Please review the following list and indicate which two statements are true.

A. Once a horse race has begun, you cannot lay down a bet, but you can do it in trading.

B. Having the background in professional gambling is a disadvantage in trading.

C. Luck can help you gamble and trade better.

D. Transaction costs are lower in the financial markets than in a casino or at the track.

E. The excitement of gambling or trading helps you focus on the game.

Question 22—Mass Psychology

When masses of traders respond to the same stimuli, their combined orders move the markets. Please review the following statements about crowd psychology and indicate which two of them are correct:

A. Markets often violate clearly visible support and resistance levels by a small margin before reversing.

B. Traders tend to hold winning positions but get out of their losses quickly.

C. Placing stops at clearly visible support and resistance levels improves profitability.

D. When the mass of traders reaches a high degree of consensus, the trend is likely to continue.

E. Professionals tend to believe that trends are driven by psychology more than economics.

Question 23—Public Opinion

People make trading decisions while bombarded by messages from mass media. Other people's views often influence us. Which two of the following statements regarding public opinion are true?

A. When a positive article about a company appears on the front page of a business journal, that stock is likely to rally much higher.

B. When the media is actively reporting a shortage of a commodity, that commodity is usually near its peak and ready to turn down.

C. When you keep hearing at parties and social gatherings that people are leaving their jobs to trade full-time, it is a sign of a healthy bull market.

D. When the media is flooded with offers to teach a new mode of trading, such as day-trading or Forex, it is likely to be a sign of a fabulous new opportunity.

E. It makes sense to check the prevailing consensus of mass media and look to go short when the crowd is overwhelmingly bullish.

Question 24—Getting Hurt by the Markets

A trader who lost a large chunk of his account in the market is likely to exhibit all of the following behaviors, except for which two?

A. Doubting his ability to find good trades

B. Blaming small account size for the inability to withstand a drawdown

C. Keeping good records to get to the root of his losses

D. Afraid to pull the trigger

E. Using money management rules for better protection

Question 25—Fear of Pulling the Trigger

Traumatized traders often become afraid to place orders. They find a stock to buy or sell short, but cannot bring themselves to execute a trade. Which two of the following statements about the fear of pulling the trigger (FPT) are true?

A. FPT is typical of inexperienced traders.

B. FPT is caused by overtrading.

C. To get over FPT, all you need is willpower.

D. To get over FPT, you need a good source of trading ideas.

E. To get over FPT, you need to trade a very small size.

Question 26—Trader's Rehab

Traders who have suffered serious losses tend to wash out from the markets. A person who decides to rehabilitate himself needs more than money to start over. He needs to change his mode of thinking and trading and develop proper record-keeping and money management. Pick three essential steps he has to take from the list below and arrange them in proper sequence:

A. Start trading a tiny size.

B. Become very critical toward himself.

C. Take a break from trading.

D. Trade markets where he has not lost money.

E. Allocate a specific amount of time to market work.

MARKETS

If trading is a battle, then the commander with a better grasp of the battlefield has an advantage over his opponent. The more you know about the market you're planning to trade, the better off you'll be. A person who puts on a trade without knowing all the key facts about that market is like a hairdresser who cuts hair without looking at his client's head. The result is likely to be ugly.

Professional traders make a point of knowing every big and little detail. They make a nice living picking up dollars and cents dropped by stumbling amateurs. If you want to succeed, you must choose a market that interests you and learn as much about it as you can.

Questions	Max. Pts. Available	Trial 1	Trial 2	Trial 3	Trial 4
27	1				
28	1				
29	1				
30	1				
31	2				
32	1				
33	1				
34	1				
35	1				
36	1				
37	1				
38	1				
Total points	13				

Question 27—A Tick

Experienced traders tend to measure price moves in ticks rather than dollars and cents. Which three of the following statements are correct?

A. A tick is a dollar

B. A tick is the smallest price change allowed in any given market.

C. A tick in e-minis is 0.25 cents.

D. A tick in a stock is always one cent.

E. A tick in corn is ⅛ of a cent.

Question 28—Stock Ideas

Which of the following are legitimate sources of stock picks?

A. Research into stock industry groups

B. Articles in the media

C. Newsletter recommendations

D. Tips heard at a party

E. All of the above

F. None of the above

Question 29—Bonds

The government decides to fight inflation by sharply raising interest rates. What will that do to the price of bonds (two possibilities)?

A. Sharply up

B. Moderately up

C. Unchanged

D. Moderately down

E. Sharply down

Question 30—Currencies

The U.S. dollar drops sharply overnight. Which of the following statements could be true of the euro at the same time (two possibilities)?

A. Has a sharp rally

B. Has a moderate rally

C. Stays unchanged

D. Has a moderate decline

E. Has a sharp decline

Question 31—Stock Industry Groups

Stocks are combined into stock industry groups by which one of the following criteria?

A. Alphabetically

B. By capitalization

C. By legal organization

D. By the type of business

E. By self-declaration to the SEC

For a bonus point: "Because of this classification, stock industry groups are identical in all databases." True or false?

Question 32—Industry Group Analysis

Please review the following statements and find a numbered set of two that is incorrect:

A. Analyzing a hundred or more groups is a proxy for analyzing thousands of stocks.

B. Tracking the number of bullish and bearish groups helps catch market bottoms and tops.

C. You trade stocks, not groups—do not waste your time doing extra work.

D. Groups change slowly, and it is not necessary to analyze them every week.

E. Group analysis is valuable only if done on a regular basis.

F. The trend of bullish and bearish groups tends to lead broad market indexes.

1. A and E
2. B and F
3. C and D
4. A and D
5. C and E

Question 33—Industry Groups and Individual Stocks

What is the preferred order of analyzing stocks and stock industry groups?

A. Analyze stocks and not groups, since you cannot trade them

B. Analyze the stock you plan to buy, confirm that its group is bullish

C. Analyze groups, look to buy for the strongest stocks in the strongest groups

D. Analyze groups, look to short the weakest stocks in the strongest group

Question 34—Trading Stocks or Options

Which of the following actions in options correspond to buying and which to shorting stocks?

A. Buying a call

B. Writing a call

C. Buying a put

D. Writing a put

Question 35—Stocks and Commodities

Please review the following statements and find a numbered set of two that is incorrect:

A. When you trade a commodity-related stock, such as a gold producer or an oil driller, it is important to analyze that commodity.

B. You are trading a stock and not a commodity—focus on what you trade and ignore the rest.

C. Gold stocks tend to follow metal prices.

D. Gold stocks tend to lead metal prices.

E. Commodity-related stocks tend to be more volatile than commodities.

1. A and C

2. B and C

3. B and D

4. C and E

5. D and E

Question 36—Futures and Options

Which of the following statements refer to options or futures, to both or neither?

A. Lower risk than stocks, higher rewards

B. Prices are dependent on the price of another product

C. Expire after a number of months

D. The prices of nearby months can rise above faraway months

E. You can walk away from a losing position

Question 37—Futures Facts

If you plan to trade futures, which of the following data must you obtain and keep current?

A. Contract size

B. Trading hours for pit and electronic trading

C. First notice day

D. Final settlement price of the previous two contracts

Choose the correct answer:

1. A

2. A and B

3. A, B, and C

4. All are correct

Question 38—Futures Rollover

When a futures contract goes off the board, the new one almost always trades at a higher or lower price, depending on the market. Trying to plot prices for the old and the new contracts on the same chart usually results in a gap, throwing off indicators. Which two statements about chart analysis during contract rollover are true?

A. Drop the old contract; start tracking the new one on a fresh chart.

B. Download the new contract into the same file as the old one and make a mental adjustment for the jump in price.

C. Download the new contract into the same file as the old one and back-adjust the old data to make it match the opening of the new contract.

D. Download a perpetual contract and use it to perform long-term analysis.

TRADING TACTICS

A piano virtuoso once said: "If I do not practice for a day, I notice my performance drop off. If I do not practice for two days, my wife notices it. If I do not practice for three days, my audience notices it." A tireless pursuit of excellence is a hallmark of a professional in any field. Trading will provide enough work to keep you busy for the rest of your life: There will always be another tool to master, another technique to learn, another method to implement. Success in trading does not depend on discovering some great secret but on a gradual improvement in your understanding and performance.

The questions in this section test how well you know the basic trading tactics. They make you focus on the markets' reactions to news and earnings announcements. These questions quiz you about the need to change trading plans under different market conditions. They test your knowledge of such basic concepts as volume and volatility, moving averages, and system trading. Whether you are a beginner or a more experienced trader, this chapter will help you measure your degree of competence in trading tactics.

Questions	Max. Pts. Available	Trial 1	Trial 2	Trial 3	Trial 4
39	1				
40	1				
41	1				
42	1				
43	1				
44	1				
45	1				
46	1				
47	1				
48	1				
49	1				
50	1				
51	1				
52	1				
53	2				
54	1				
55	1				
56	1				
57	1				
58	1				
Total points	21				

Question 39—Trading and News

Your weekend analysis of weekly and daily charts indicates that a certain stock has topped out and is ready to be shorted. On Monday, before the market opens, there is a report on a financial news network that the company plans a strategic acquisition; the expert on your favorite financial Web site sees it doubling within two years and recommends using dips for buying. Which three of the following actions would make sense?

A. Short as planned.

B. Stand aside to reevaluate the situation as the week progresses.

C. Change the plan and look for a buying opportunity.

D. Search other financial Web sites and rate their consensus.

E. Short half the size you had planned.

Question 40—Changing Trading Plans

The stock you bought for $31.30, with a target of 36 and a stop at 29, sank to 30.17 as the market dropped by the end of the day. What is the advised course of action?

A. Continue to hold according to the plan.

B. Add to the position, taking advantage of lower prices.

C. Get out at the opening tomorrow.

D. Raise the stop to 30.

E. Pay for a consultation with an expert.

Question 41—Changed Market Conditions

The stock you bought has been moving in your favor for several days but then developed tremendous volatility, with unexpectedly large swings. Which of the following approaches would make sense?

A. Maintain your stop and profit targets as planned, and stay away from the screen.

B. Exit the unexpectedly volatile market and reevaluate from the sidelines.

C. Zoom in on intraday charts.

D. Review additional indicators you haven't used yet.

1. A

2. A and B

3. A, B, and C

4. All are correct

Question 42—Trading Earnings

Publicly traded companies release a steady stream of earnings reports. Their dates are known in advance, and many fundamental analysts make their buy or sell recommendations on the basis of company earnings. Which two of the following five statements are true?

A. Volatility tends to jump as earnings are released.

B. You should never trade for a few days prior to and following earnings releases.

C. Since earnings are fundamental factors, a technical trader can ignore them.

D. Stocks rise after positive and fall after negative earnings reports.

E. A strong technical buy or sell signal just prior to earnings report should be traded.

Question 43—Trading at the Time of a Disaster

A massive natural disaster hits the economy and the financial markets. Which three of the following statements are true?

A. Expect increased volatility.

B. Expect bonds to rise.

C. Expect stocks to fall.

D. Close out all open positions.

E. Reduce your trading size.

Question 44—Classical Charting

The instruments of classical charting in pre-computer days were rulers, colored pencils, and protractors. Today classical charting is included in computer programs, and an analyst may use a mouse to draw a trendline or mark a zone of support or resistance. Classical charting has its advantages and disadvantages compared to computerized analysis. Please review the list of statements below and identify the three correct ones:

A. Classical charting should not be combined with any other methods.

B. The simplicity of classical charting keeps you closer to the real market.

C. Classical charting is more subjective than computerized charting.

D. A trendline break provides a decisive signal of trend change.

E. It makes little difference whether you draw trendlines across the extreme points or the edges of congestion zones, as long as you are consistent.

Question 45—Price-Volume Analysis

Changes in prices and volume reflect shifts in buying and selling. While there are no hard-and-fast rules, some patterns of price and volume can help you decide whether the current trend is likely to continue or to reverse. Please review the following descriptions and indicate which two patterns are more likely to lead to a reversal and which two to a continuation of the current trend:

A. A rally, a tall bar, followed by a short and stunted bar

B. A rally, a tall bar, closing near the high

C. A decline, a narrow range day with high volume

D. A breakout below the previous low, tall bar, high volume

Question 46—Trading Gap Openings

While doing your homework on a weekend, you find a $19 stock in a well-established uptrend. It has been in a narrow range for the past few days, and you decide to buy, expecting the uptrend to resume. You decide to buy on Monday in the vicinity of the Friday's close, with a profit target three points above and a stop-loss one point below. On Monday morning the stock opens one dollar above the Friday's high and continues to rise intraday. What are the two things you may do?

A. Buy what you planned—your forecast of an uptrend was correct, get in.

B. Stand aside—you missed the entry; look for trades elsewhere.

C. Recalculate your risk; buy at the market, but smaller size.

D. Place a buy order as planned—get the stock if it comes back to you.

E. Strike this stock from your list and never look at it again.

Question 47—Trending and Non-Trending Markets

Uptrends and downtrends attract us whenever we look at a chart. Taking a closer look, we notice a lot of backing and filling between the upmoves and downmoves. Please review the following statements and indicate the three correct ones:

A. Markets spend more time moving sideways than up or down.

B. Flat markets and rapidly moving markets call for different trading tactics.

C. A good system adjusts to transitions between flat and moving markets.

D. Flat markets are more forgiving and easier to trade than trending markets.

E. Daily ranges always become more narrow whenever a market shifts from a non-trending to a trending mode.

Question 48—Volatility

Prices of some stocks change slowly, while others swing all over the lot. Since traders look to profit from price changes, volatility—the degree of price change over a period of time—is an important factor in their success or failure. Please review the following statements about volatility and indicate the two correct ones:

A. A volatile stock is always volatile, and a stock with low volatility always stays that way.

B. Periods of high volatility are the best for entering trades.

C. A stock normally oscillates between periods of high and low volatility.

D. Catching a transition from low to high volatility and vice versa can provide a useful trading signal.

E. When a standard deviation channel (Bollinger bands) squeezes prices, it is a good time to exit a trade.

Question 49—Long-Term Chart Patterns

Traders deal with shorter-term patterns, while investors prefer to study longer-term charts. Which two of the following statements regarding long-term patterns are correct?

A. If a stock sat in a trading range for more than five years, it is unlikely to break out.

B. Stocks that rallied early in one bull market are likely to rally early in the next bull market.

C. The longer the trading range, the greater the likely extent of a trend after a breakout.

D. If a stock pulls back into its range following a breakout, it provides a good buying opportunity.

E. Trying to catch long-term trends requires being ready to take extra-large losses.

Question 50—Moving Average Signals

Which three of the following statements about exponential moving averages are correct?

A. An upturn of a flat EMA gives a buy signal.

B. A return of prices to a falling EMA gives a shorting signal.

C. Prices rallying to a record distance above an EMA forecast higher prices ahead.

D. The area between a fast and a slow EMA is the sweet zone for entering trades.

E. The shorter an EMA, the more reliable its signals.

Question 51—Tomorrow's Moving Average

You find a stock in an uptrend and decide to go long. You want to buy at or below value, as reflected by the EMA. If you do your homework in the evening, how can you tell where the EMA will be tomorrow?

A. You won't know that level until the stock opens—wait to place your order until after the opening.

B. That level can fluctuate intraday—wait to place your order until five minutes before the close.

C. Use today's EMA level as a proxy for tomorrow's level.

D. Calculate the difference between the EMA for the past two days and add that number to today's EMA.

Question 52—Trading Channels

A channel or an envelope runs parallel to a moving average and contains approximately 95% of recent prices. When the crowd becomes especially bullish, prices break out of the channel to the upside; prices break out to the downside when the crowd becomes especially bearish. Which three of the following statements about channels are true?

A. Prices give buy signals when they rally out of their channel.

B. When prices break down from their channel they give a signal to trade short.

C. Channels provide attractive profit targets.

D. The portion of channel height captured in a trade is a good measurement of the trader's performance.

E. A divergence of a technical indicator when prices hit their channel wall warns of a reversal.

Question 53—Hierarchy of Indicators

Some indicator patterns are more important than others. If we look at the same timeframe, which of the following patterns belong to the first order of importance and which to the second?

A. Stochastic overbought/oversold

B. The trend of the moving average

C. A divergence of MACD-Histogram

D. Force Index above or below zero

E. Price outside the envelope

Bonus question: Are these patterns more important on daily or weekly charts?

Question 54—Impulse Exit

If you enter a trade using the Impulse system, all of the following exits could be legitimate, except for which one?

A. Exit when prices hit your price target.

B. Exit when the trade violates the 2% Rule.

C. Exit when prices hit a stop.

D. Exit when the Impulse color is in favor of your trade.

E. Exit when the Impulse color turns against your trade.

Question 55—Developing a System

"Developing a trading system is part art, part science, and part common sense," wrote Fred Schutzman in an e-mail following his interview. He outlined the five-step process he and his business partner use to develop trading systems. The order of these steps is scrambled below— please arrange them in a logical sequence.

1. Visually check out the signals on the charts.

2. Formally test the system with a computer.

3. Start with a concept.

4. Evaluate the results.

5. Turn the concept into a set of objective rules.

Question 56—System Trading

The seemingly unemotional nature of system trading appeals to many people. Researching the markets, coming up with a set of rules, back-testing them, and putting the system on autopilot may reduce the stress level. Which three of the following statements about system trading are correct?

A. You must trade all signals of your system, whether you like them or not.

B. It does not matter on what concept the system is based, as long as it is profitable in backtesting.

C. A system trader has little interest in the outcome of any single trade.

D. A system must include a rule when to stop trading that system.

E. A well-designed and well-tested system will produce steady profits in the future.

Question 57—Writing Options

If you sell a naked put, and the stock starts going down, which three of the following courses of action would make sense?

A. Monitor your profit.

B. Short the stock.

C. Buy the stock.

D. Sell a call.

E. Buy a put.

Question 58—Effective Volume and Active Boundaries

The interview with Pascal Willain in *Entries & Exits* marked the first public presentation of his method. Please review these two sets of statements, one numbered and the other lettered, and match each lettered line to a numbered line:

A. Dividing a stock's daily action into one-minute segments

B. A one-minute bar that has more than 10% of that day's volume

C. Effective Volume

D. Active Boundaries

E. Large Effective Volume

1. Reflects a block trade and should be eliminated

2. Isolating volume that leads to price changes

3. A volume-based indicator of overbought and oversold conditions

4. Effective volume above the midpoint for the day

5. A portion of a minute's volume responsible for price change

MONEY MANAGEMENT AND RECORD-KEEPING

Many years ago, well before I discovered the importance of money management, it puzzled me to no end why I could make so many successful trades but could not grow my equity. Now we know that putting too much money at risk exposes you to unacceptable dangers in trading. Now we have specific rules designed to protect any size account. This chapter asks you several questions about those rules.

Many traders interviewed in *Entries & Exits* said that the turning point in their trading life came after they began keeping good records. Whenever you put on a trade, you should have two goals—to make money and to become a better trader. Your records are designed to help you learn from your experience, instead of running in endless circles.

Questions	Max. Pts. Available	Trial 1	Trial 2	Trial 3	Trial 4
59	1				
60	1				
61	1				
62	1				
63	1				
64	1				
65	1				
66	1				
67	1				
68	1				
69	1				
Total points	11				

Question 59—Trade Size

A trader with a $74,000 account discovers a $7 stock that he expects will rise sharply within a few months. He also thinks that a closing below $6 would violate major support, and plans to put in a hard stop at $5.60. The maximum number of shares he may buy is:

A. 200 shares

B. 1,000 shares

C. 10,000 shares

D. 20,000 shares on margin

Question 60—Changing Trade Size

To follow up on the previous question, a trader decides to trade a different number of shares. Which three of the following options are legitimate?

A. Buy 900 shares.

B. Go on margin and buy 2,000 shares, since it is the broker's money that will be at risk.

C. Buy 500 shares.

D. Buy 100 shares, just to test this trading idea.

Question 61—The 6% Rule

A trader with a $74,000 account is having a good month. He is holding three positions that have moved nicely in his favor, allowing him to raise his stops to breakeven. He also has three additional positions, risking $1,200 in each of them. He sees a highly attractive trading opportunity, and wants to buy 1,000 shares of an $8 stock, putting a stop at $7. Which of the following statements is true?

A. Go ahead—his risk is under 2%.

B. Stand aside—he is maxed out on his permitted risk.

C. Increase the size of the trade.

D. Reduce the size of the trade.

Question 62—Okay to Add?

A trader starts the month with $52,000. His first trade is a breakeven, but then he takes two losses of $700 and $800. After a brief pause, he buys 1,000 shares of an $11.50 stock with a stop at $10.50 and 200 shares of a $21 stock with a stop at $19.50. He then discovers a $7 stock that looks more promising than all of that month's picks combined, with a tight stop that belongs at $6.50. Since the 2% Rule allows him to risk a bit over $1,000 per trade, he wants to buy 2,000 shares. Would that be a legal trade?

Question 63—Legal or Not?

Which three of these trades are permitted under the 2% Rule and which three would violate it?

A. $20,000 account. Long a stock at 27.30, stop at 25.90; plan to buy 500 shares.

B. $80,000 account. Sell short a stock at 77.90, stop at 81.00; plan to short 500 shares.

C. $120,000 account. Buy a stock at 18.20, stop at 17.20; plan to buy 3,000 shares.

D. $200,000 account. Buy a stock at 3.90, stop at 3.50; plan to buy 8,000 shares.

E. $400,000 account. Buy a stock at 7.80, stop at 7.40; plan to buy 15,000 shares.

F. $1,200,000 account. Sell short a stock at 285.30, stop at 302; plan to short 2,000 shares.

Question 64—A Trader's Spreadsheet

Which of the following data must be recorded in the spreadsheet for tracking your trades?

A. Date and price of entry and exit

B. Position size

C. Commissions

D. Slippage

E. Levels of broad market indexes

Choose the correct answer:

1. A

2. A and B

3. A, B, and C

4. A, B, C, and D

5. All are correct

Question 65—Trader's Diary

Some traders keep a diary in addition to a spreadsheet, where they record the details of their trades. Which two of the following statements regarding a trader's diary are correct?

A. Do not waste your time—look forward instead of backward.

B. Print out the charts and mark up entry and exit signals.

C. Add notes about your feelings to technical signals.

D. Use your diary to record only your best trades.

Question 66—Rating a Trade

To measure your performance in any given trade, in addition to total profit or loss, which two additional ratings are useful?

A. The percentage gain of the stock market's best performing stock during your trade

B. The percentage of the height of the trading channel captured in your trade

C. The performance of your worst stock while you were in this trade

D. The position of entry and exit prices within the high-low range of the entry and exit days

Question 67—Trade Grade

The method for grading trades, suggested in *Come into My Trading Room*, is to compare profit per stock per trade to the height of the channel. If you use a combination of weekly and daily charts, the channel on the dailies provides the yardstick. Capturing 30% or more earns you an A, 20 to 30% a B, 10 to 20% a C, and below that a D. Please review the following trades and rate them:

1. Buy XYZ at $18.50, sell at $20. Daily channel $22 to $16

2. Buy ZYX at $41, sell at $39.50. Daily channel $44 to $36

3. Short YXZ at $89, cover at $83. Daily channel $95 to $77

4. Short YZX at $52, cover at $51. Daily channel $54 to $46

Question 68—Weekend Homework

A trader spends several hours each weekend reviewing potential trades for the week ahead. Which of the following records are worth keeping on a weekly basis?

A. Ratings of key market indexes, whether bullish, bearish, or neutral

B. Ratings of stock industry groups, whether bullish, bearish, or neutral

C. An earnings calendar for the stocks he is considering trading

D. A list of key fundamental announcements for the coming week

Choose the correct answer:

1. A

2. A and B

3. A, B, and C

4. All are correct

Question 69—Preparing to Enter

A trader doing his homework finds two stocks that he decides to buy the following day. Which three of the following approaches to implementing his plan are acceptable and which three are not?

A. Transmit an electronic limit order. After receiving a fill, place both a stop order and a "take profit" order OCO—one cancels other.

B. Transmit an electronic limit order. After receiving a fill, place a stop and watch prices to take profits if your broker does not accept OCO orders.

C. Transmit an electronic limit order. After receiving a fill, place a "take profit" order and watch your stop level if your broker does not accept OCO orders.

D. Write down your planned entry level, stop, and profit target. Give your orders to the broker after the opening.

E. Write down your planned entry level, stop, and profit target. Enter at the market if the stock opens above the planned entry.

F. Memorize your planned entry level, stop, and profit target. Give your orders to the broker after the opening.

CASE STUDIES

Most of these case studies were suggested by traders interviewed in *Entries & Exits*. This section gives you an opportunity to revisit their trading rooms and find out how well you have learned their methods.

Each case study shows you one or two charts and asks you to identify their signals and make a trading decision. Many answers feature an additional chart, showing how that trade worked out. Do not rush, take your time working with these case studies. They are designed to help you better understand how serious traders make their decisions.

Questions	Max. Pts. Available	Trial 1	Trial 2	Trial 3	Trial 4
70	3				
71	2				
72	2				
73	2				
74	1				
75	2				
76	3				
77	2				
78	2				
79	2				
80	2				
81	1				
82	2				
83	2				
84	2				
85	3				
86	2				
87	3				
88	2				
89	2				
90	2				
91	2				
92	1				
93	1				
94	2				
Total points	50				

Question 70—Moving Averages and Trend Reversals

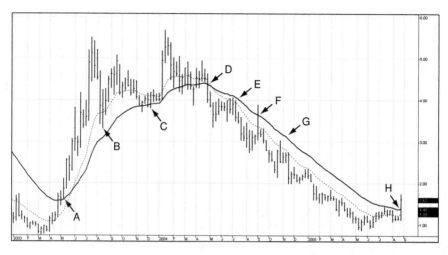

Figure 6.70 Weekly bar chart with 26- and 13-week exponential moving averages.

Please review EMA signals, marked with letters on Figure 6.70, and assign each to group 1 or 2.

Group 1—confirms trend reversals (one point)

Group 2—identifies value zone entries (one point)

For a bonus point: Identify a kangaroo tail (also called a finger).

Question 71—MACD-Histogram

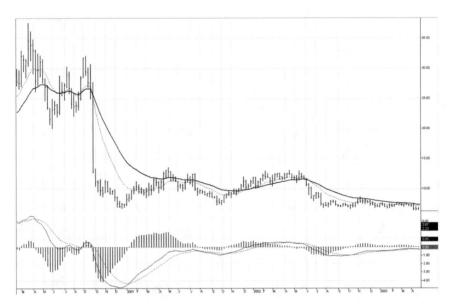

Figure 6.71-1 Upper pane—weekly bar chart with 26- and 13-week exponential moving averages. Lower pane—12-26-9 MACD-Lines and MACD-Histogram.

The stock collapsed in September 2000, driven down by a bad earnings surprise. MACD-Histogram fell to a new low, warning of even lower prices ahead. It traded at those low levels for over two years after its collapse, acting like a man who falls out of a high window and just lies on the ground, convulsing a little and trying to breathe. There were serious questions in the financial media whether the company would be able to continue as a going concern. At the right edge of Figure 6.71-1 everything is in gear to the downside. The price has just broken down to a new low. Both EMAs are declining, confirming the downtrend. MACD-Histogram is declining, showing that the dominant market crowd is pushing down.

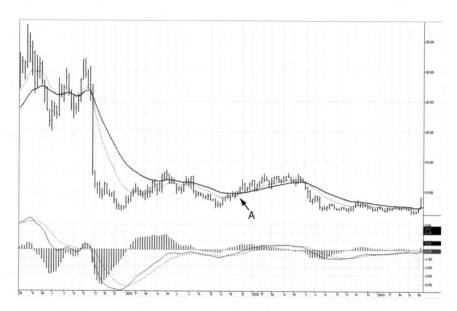

Figure 6.71-2

Two weeks later there are several new developments. Which three statements regarding the right edge of Figure 6.71-2 are correct?

A. A false downside breakout

B. A pullback in a downtrend

C. A confirmation of the downtrend

D. A bullish divergence of MACD-Histogram

E. A bullish divergence of MACD-Lines

For a bonus point: Identify the pattern at point A.

Question 72—Force Index

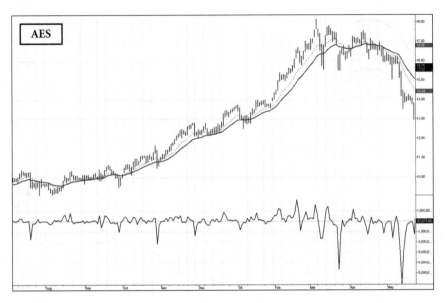

Figure 6.72-1 Upper pane—daily bar chart with 22- and 13-day EMAs and 2.7 standard deviation Autoenvelope. Lower pane—2-day EMA of Force Index.

AES, an electric utility company, had a nice run in 2004 and 2005, when interest rates were falling. As the Fed began to tighten, AES, which by then had nearly doubled, started to decline, along with most companies in that group. At the right edge of Figure 6.72-1, AES has just broken down to a new low, on surging volume. Its moving average is down, confirming the downtrend.

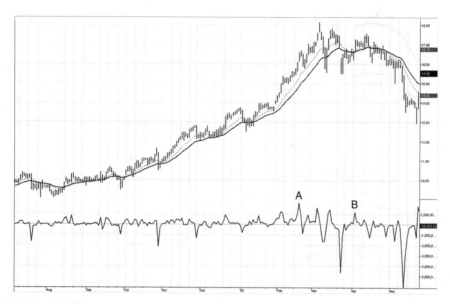

Figure 6.72-2

The break to a new low was followed by a rally the following day. Near the right edge of Figure 6.72-2, which four of the following statements are correct?

A. A spike of Force Index

B. A false downside breakout

C. A bullish divergence

D. A bearish divergence

E. If going long, place a stop near 13.50

F. If going long, place a stop near 13

For a bonus point: Identify the pattern in area A—B.

Question 73—Weekly and Daily Impulse

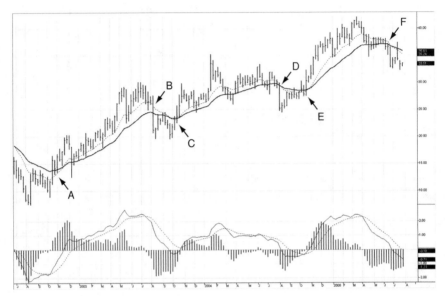

Figure 6.73-1 Upper pane—weekly bar chart with 26- and 13-week EMAs. Lower pane—MACD-Lines and MACD-Histogram 12-26-9.

Figure 6.73-1, together with the daily chart (Figure 6.73-2) that follows, shows the search for a trade at the right edge. Please review the stock's history and match each letter or group of letters on the weekly chart to the following descriptions.

1. EMA becomes bullish.

2. EMA becomes bearish.

At the right edge of the weekly chart (Figure 6.73-1), both EMAs are falling and MACD-Histogram is rising. Which of the following statements about the Impulse system are true?

3. Buying is permitted.

4. Standing aside is permitted.

5. Shorting is permitted.

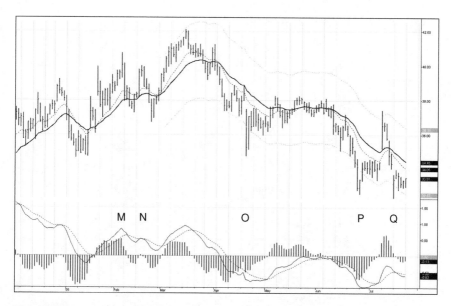

Figure 6.73-2 Upper pane—daily bar chart with 22- and 13-day EMAs. Lower pane—MACD-Lines and MACD-Histogram 12-26-9.

Please identify the areas on the daily chart (Figure 6.73-2) that correspond to the following patterns.

1. A bullish divergence

2. A spike reversal

3. A bearish divergence

Which statement regarding the right edge of Figure 6.73-2 is true?

4. With the weekly chart permitting shorting and the daily EMAs down, go short.

5. With the weekly Impulse permitting buying and the daily MACD bullish, go long.

6. Stand aside.

Question 74—Looking for a Day-Trade

Figure 6.74 Upper pane—5-minute candlestick chart with 20-bar SMA and 20-bar Bollinger band. Second pane—MACD-Lines and MACD-Histogram 12-26-9. Third pane—10-bar Momentum. Bottom pane—10-4-4 Slow Stochastic.

Figure 6.74 reflects one trader's search for a day-trade. Please answer questions regarding the right edge of the chart:

A. Is the trend up or down?

B. Is volatility increasing or decreasing?

C. How many indicators show bullish or bearish divergences?

D. Does the balance of the evidence favor a long or a short?

Question 75—Commodities

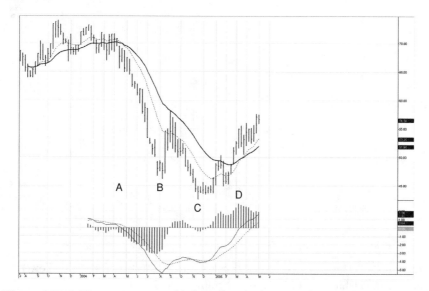

Figure 6.75-1 Upper pane—weekly bar chart with 26- and 13-week EMAs. Lower pane—MACD-Lines and MACD-Histogram 12-26-9.

Figure 6.75-1, together with the daily chart that follows (Figure 6.75-2), reflects the search for a trade at the right edge. Please review this commodity's history and match each letter or group of letters to the following descriptions.

1. EMA becomes bullish.

2. EMA becomes bearish.

3. A bullish divergence.

At the right edge of the weekly chart (Figure 6.75-1), the EMAs are rising and MACD-Histogram is falling. Which of the following statements about the Impulse system are correct?

4. Buying is permitted.

5. Standing aside is permitted.

6. Shorting is permitted.

Figure 6.75-2 Upper pane—daily bar chart with 22- and 13-day EMAs. Lower pane—MACD-Lines and MACD-Histogram 12-26-9.

Please identify the areas on Figure 6.75-2 that correspond to the following patterns.

1. An EMA buy

2. An EMA sell

3. A bearish divergence

4. Pullbacks to value

Which of the following statements regarding the right edge of Figure 6.75-2 are correct?

5. With the weekly Impulse permitting shorting the daily patterns suggest going short.

6. With the weekly Impulse permitting buying the daily patterns suggest going long.

7. Stand aside.

Question 76—Charting

Figure 6.76-1 Upper pane—weekly candlestick chart. Middle pane—MACD-Histogram 12-26-9. Lower pane—volume.

Figure 6.76-1, together with the daily chart that follows (Figure 6.76-2), reflects a search for a trade at the right edge. Please review wheat's history and identify the following patterns.

1. A bullish divergence

2. A bearish divergence

3. False breakouts

4. Rally runs into resistance at a trendline

5. Decline finds support at a trendline

Figure 6.76-2 Upper pane—daily candlestick chart. Middle pane—MACD-Histogram 12-26-9. Lower pane—volume.

Please identify the areas on Figure 6.76-2 that correspond to the following patterns.

1. A bearish divergence

2. A bullish divergence

3. Spike tops

4. Decline finds support at a trendline

5. Rally runs into resistance at a trendline

Make a trading decision: After reviewing both the weekly and daily chart, would you like to go long or go short? Explain.

Question 77—Channels and Divergences

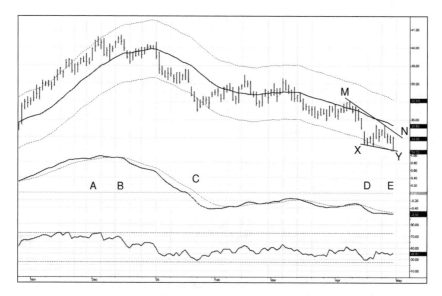

Figure 6.77 Upper pane—daily bar chart with 21-bar SMA and ± 4% envelope. Second pane—MACD-Lines 19-39-9. Bottom pane—14-day RSI.

Figure 6.77 reflects a search for a swing trade. Please identify the following patterns and answer questions regarding the right edge of the chart. Give yourself a point for answering correctly.

1. Identify a bearish divergence of the RSI and/or MACD.

2. Identify a bullish divergence of the RSI and/or MACD.

3. Identify zones where prices are extremely undervalued.

4. What is the name of the pattern bordered by lines M-N and X-Y?

Make a trading decision: At the right edge does the balance of the evidence favor a long or a short? Explain. Give yourself a bonus point for answering correctly.

Question 78—Trading Plans: A New High

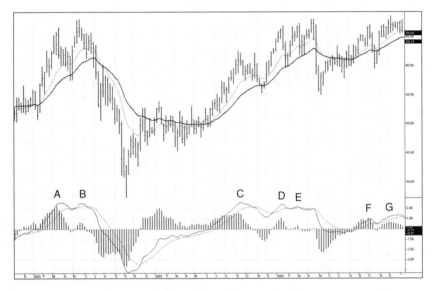

Figure 6.78-1 Upper pane—weekly bar chart with 26- and 13-week EMAs. Lower pane—MACD-Lines and MACD-Histogram 12-26-9.

Figure 6.78-1, together with the daily chart that follows (Figure 6.78-2), shows the search for a trade at the right edge. Please review the stock's history and indicate which four of the following statements are correct. Give yourself a point for answering correctly.

1. Points B, E, and G are new highs in an uptrend.

2. Patterns A-B, C-D-E, and F-G are bearish divergences between prices and MACD-Histogram.

3. Points B, E, and G are false breakouts to a new high.

4. At the right edge of the chart, two rising EMAs give a buy signal.

5. At the right edge of the chart, the pattern of MACD-Histogram and a false breakout to a new high give a sell signal.

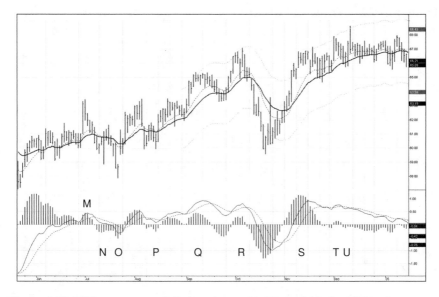

Figure 6.78-2 Upper pane—daily bar chart with 22- and 13-day EMAs. Lower pane—MACD-Lines and MACD-Histogram 12-26-9.

This daily chart (Figure 6.78-2) ends on the same day as the weekly (Figure 6.78-1). Even though the strategic decision is made on the weekly chart, it is important to examine the daily chart to see whether its signals confirm the weekly. Please review the stock's history and indicate which three of the following statements are correct. Give yourself a point for answering correctly.

6. Points M and U are spike reversals.

7. Patterns N-O and P-Q are bullish divergences.

8. Patterns Q-R and S-T are bearish divergences.

9. At the right edge of the screen, a minor bullish divergence of MACD-Histogram gives a buy signal.

10. At the right edge of the screen, the downturn of the EMAs gives a sell signal.

Question 79—Trading Volatility

Figure 6.79 Upper pane—daily bar chart with 20-day SMA (simple moving average) and 20-day Bollinger bands. Lower pane—MACD-Lines and MACD-Histogram 12-26-9.

Volatility—the change of price per unit of time—is an essential characteristic of any market, closely watched by professional traders. Please identify the areas on Figure 6.79 bracketed by two letters (such as A-B) that correspond to the following patterns. Give yourself a point for answering correctly.

1. Low volatility

2. High volatility

3. Bullish divergence

Which one of the following statements regarding the right edge of Figure 6.79 is true? Give yourself a point for answering correctly.

4. Sell short at the right edge of the chart.

5. Buy long at the right edge of the chart.

6. Place a buy stop order above $10 level.

7. Place a shorting order below $9 level.

Question 80—A Big Base

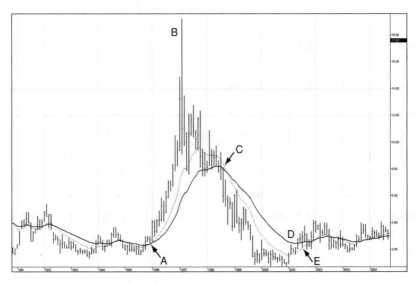

Figure 6.80 Monthly bar chart with 26- and 13-months EMAs

This monthly chart spans 13 years and shows several stages in the life of this stock. It was flat, between $2 and $4 for several years until it woke up in 1996 and flew up to $19. The period prior to that bull market may look flat in retrospect, but remember that during those swings between $2 and $4 the stock kept doubling in price and then giving up its gains. An upturn of the moving average, A, caught the onset of the bull market, but the downturn, C, was less timely; it occurred after the stock lost more than half of its value. In area D, the stock broke down to a new low but the breakout had no follow-through; an upturn of the EMA at E marked the end of the bear market. Which four of the following statements about the right edge of Figure 6.80 are correct?

A. There is a trading range between $2 and $4.

B. The trend is bullish—the EMA is rising.

C. The rally from the 2000 low has run into resistance at $4.

D. Be prepared to buy an upside breakout above $4.

E. Be prepared to short a downside breakout below $2.

For a bonus point: Identify the chart pattern at point B.

Question 81—Price-Volume Behavior

Cover Figure 6.81 with a sheet of paper and move it slowly from left to right, evaluating each price and volume bar in relation to the previous bars. The date and price markings have been removed to help you focus on the universal features of this chart. You should be able to recognize several fairly common price patterns. Several bars have been marked by letters. Please find each lettered day that corresponds to a number below.

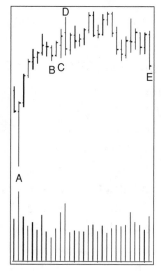

Figure 6.81 Upper pane—daily bar chart. Lower pane—volume.

1. A rally confirmed by volume—bulls win the day

2. A failed rally

3. A kangaroo tail

4. A decline confirmed by volume—bears win the day

5. An unconfirmed decline

Question 82—Trading Plans: Long, Short, or Stand Aside?

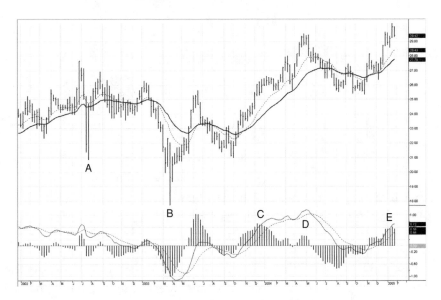

Figure 6.82-1 Upper pane—weekly bar chart with 26- and 13-week EMAs. Lower pane—MACD-Lines and MACD-Histogram 12-26-9.

The weekly chart, together with the daily chart that follows (Figure 6.82-2), reflects the search for a trade at the right edge. Please review the stock's history and match each letter or group of letters to the following descriptions. Give yourself a point for answering correctly.

1. A kangaroo tail or a spike reversal

2. A bearish divergence

3. A false breakout to a new high

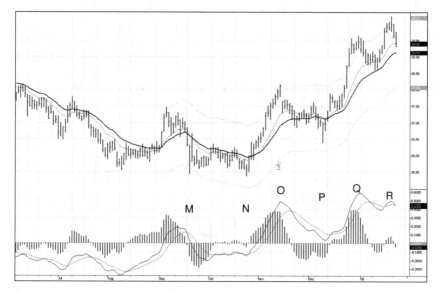

Figure 6.82-2 Upper pane—daily bar chart with 22- and 13-day EMAs. Lower pane—MACD- Lines and MACD-Histogram 12-26-9.

This daily chart (Figure 6.82-2) ends on the same day as the weekly (Figure 6.82-1). Even though the strategic decision is made on the basis of the weekly chart, it is important to examine the daily and see whether it confirms the weekly signals. Please review the stock's history and match each letter or group of letters to the following descriptions. Give yourself a point for answering correctly.

1. A bullish divergence

2. A kangaroo tail

3. A bearish divergence

4. A false breakout to a new low

5. At the right edge—go long or short?

Question 83—A Squeeze Play

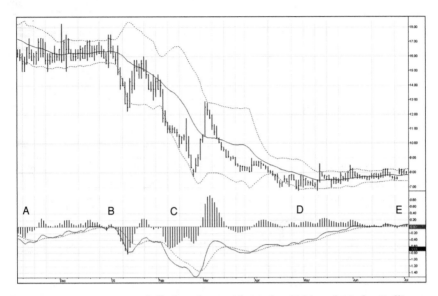

Figure 6.83 Upper pane—daily bar chart with 20-day SMA and 20-day Bollinger bands. Lower pane—MACD-Lines and MACD-Histogram 12-26-9.

Anyone can base his trade on a change in price, but it takes a pro to take advantage of a change in volatility. Please identify the areas bracketed by two letters (such as A-B) that correspond to the following patterns. Give yourself a point for answering correctly.

1. Low volatility

2. High volatility

3. Bullish divergence

Give yourself a point for making the correct choice:

4. Go long at the market at the right edge of the chart.

5. Place a buy stop order above $8.50 level.

6. Go short at the market at the right edge of the chart.

7. Place a shorting order below $7 level.

Question 84—Looking for a Position Trade

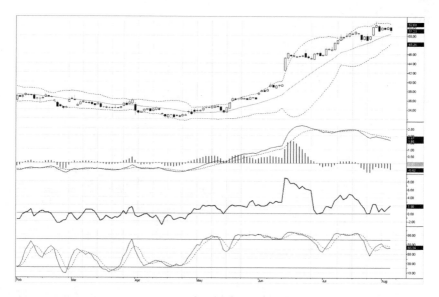

Figure 6.84 Upper pane—daily candlestick chart with 20-bar SMA and 20-bar Bollinger band. Second pane—MACD-Lines and MACD-Histogram 12-26-9. Third pane—10-bar Momentum. Bottom pane—10-4-4 Slow Stochastic.

Figure 6.84 reflects one trader's search for a position trade. Please answer questions regarding the right edge of the chart and make a trading decision. Give yourself a point for answering correctly.

A. Is the trend up or down?

B. Is volatility increasing or decreasing?

C. How many indicators show bullish or bearish divergences?

Make a trading decision: Does the balance of the evidence favor a long or a short? Give yourself a point for answering correctly.

Question 85—Away from Value

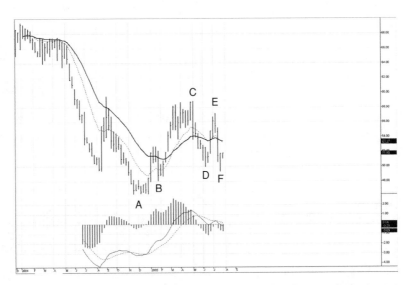

Figure 6.85-1 Upper pane—weekly bar chart with 26- and 13-week EMAs. Lower pane—MACD-Lines and MACD-Histogram 12-26-9.

Figure 6.85-1, together with the daily chart that follows (Figure 6.85-2), reflects the search for a trade at the right edge. Please review cotton's history and answer the following questions. Give yourself a point for answering correctly.

1. If the distance from the EMA to the price peak identifies the ability of bulls to stretch prices away from value, at which peak are bulls weaker than at the previous peak?

2. If the distance from the EMA to the bottom identifies the ability of bears to stretch prices away from value, at which low are bears weaker than at the previous low?

3. At the right edge of the chart, is cotton overvalued, undervalued, or fairly valued?

4. At the right edge, does the weekly Impulse permit buying, shorting, or standing aside?

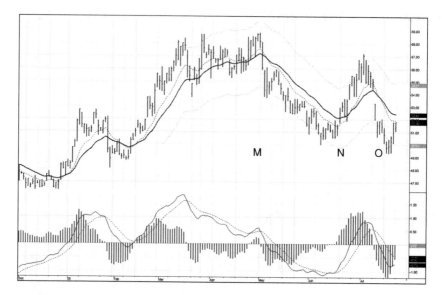

Figure 6.85-2 Upper pane—daily bar chart with 22- and 13-day EMAs. Lower pane—MACD-Lines and MACD-Histogram 12-26-9.

Please identify the areas on Figure 6.85-2 that correspond to the following patterns. Give yourself a point for answering correctly.

1. An EMA buy

2. An EMA sell

3. A false upside breakout

Make a trading decision and give yourself a point for answering correctly.

4. With the weekly Impulse permitting shorting the daily patterns suggest going short.

5. With the weekly Impulse permitting buying the daily patterns suggest going long.

6. The weekly and daily Impulse are in conflict—stand aside.

Question 86—Moving Averages and False Breakouts

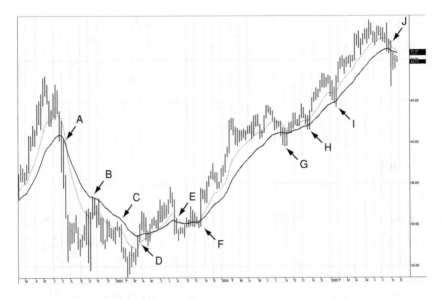

Figure 6.86 Weekly bar chart with 26- and 13-week exponential moving averages.

Please review EMA signals marked on Figure 6.86 and assign each to group 1 or 2.

Group 1—confirms trend reversals

Group 2—identifies value zone entries

For a bonus point: Identify a false downward breakout.

Question 87—Charting a Currency

Figure 6.87-1 Upper pane—weekly candlestick chart. Middle pane—MACD-Histogram 12-26-9. Lower pane—volume.

This weekly chart, together with the daily chart that follows (Figure 6.87-2), shows the search for a trade at the right edge. Please review this chart and identify the following patterns. Give yourself a point for answering correctly.

1. A rally tops out at a resistance level

2. A decline ends at a support level

3. A double top with a false upside breakout

4. A "missing right shoulder" bearish divergence

Figure 6.87-2 Upper pane—daily candlestick chart. Middle pane—MACD-Histogram 12-26-9. Lower pane—volume.

Please identify the areas on Figure 6.87-2 that correspond to the following patterns. Give yourself a point for answering correctly.

1. A bullish divergence

2. The first downtrendline is established

3. The second downtrendline is established

4. The second downtrendline is broken

Make a trading decision: After reviewing both the weekly and daily charts, are you inclined to go long or go short? Explain. Give yourself a bonus point for answering correctly.

Question 88—Potential and Actual Breaks

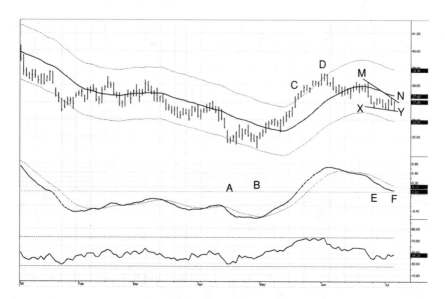

Figure 6.88 Upper pane—daily bar chart with 21-bar SMA and ± 4% envelope. Second pane—MACD-Lines 19-39-9. Bottom pane—14-day RSI.

Figure 6.88 reflects a search for a swing trade. Please identify the following patterns, answer questions regarding the right edge of the chart, and make a trading decision.

1. Strongly undervalued

2. An actual and/or potential bullish divergence

3. Strongly overvalued

4. An actual and/or potential false breakdown to a new low

5. At the right edge, does the balance of the evidence favor a long or a short? Explain.

For a bonus point: Explain the difference between an actual and potential breakdown.

Question 89—Market Consensus

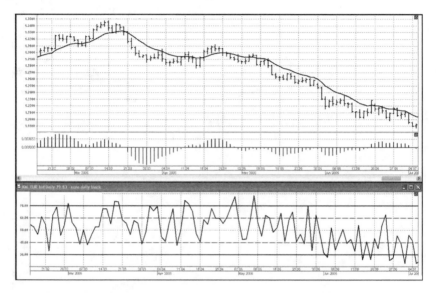

Figure 6.89 Upper pane—daily bar chart with 12-day EMA. Second pane—MACD-Histogram 12-26-9. Bottom pane—Forex Club Sentiment Index (FCSI).

Please insert the word "up" or "down" into the following statements regarding the right edge of Figure 6.89:

1. The trend of the EMA is _____.

2. The slope of MACD-Histogram is _____.

3. The bullish consensus of the mass of traders, at 23, shows that the majority expects this market to go _____.

4. FCSI suggests shorting or buying?

Bonus question: If you were to enter a trade based on FCSI at the right edge of the chart, will you enter at the market on a break through the extreme of the previous bar?

Question 90—MACD-Histogram

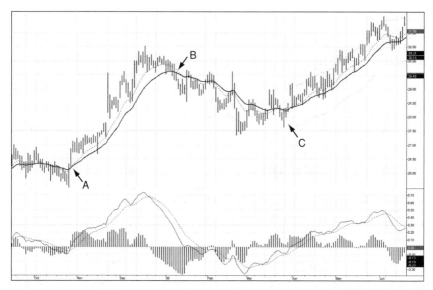

Figure 6.90-1 Upper pane—daily bar chart with 22- and 13-day EMAs and 2.7 standard deviation Autoenvelope. Lower pane—12-26-9 MACD-Lines and MACD-Histogram.

The upturns and downturns of the EMA did a good job of identifying uptrends and downtrends of this stock. At the same, you can see a lack of smoothness and even some jerkiness of the EMA line—a sign that its period is a little too short. When you track many stocks, you have to select an EMA length and stay with it, but if you track just a handful of issues, you can individually tailor an EMA for each one.

At the right edge of a chart a trader must ask: Am I a bull, a bear, or undecided? In Figure 6.90-1 you can see several bullish signs, primarily the uptrend of the EMA and a rising MACD-Histogram. At the same time, there are bearish signs—a possible double top as prices hit their upper channel line and a suspiciously deep bottom of MACD-Histogram during the latest decline. Experienced traders look for clear signals and stand aside when markets give them conflicting messages.

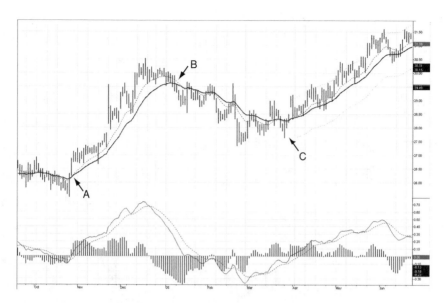

Figure 6.90-2 (updated three days later)

The stock has been boiling for three days since the previous chart (Figure 6.90-1). At the right edge of Figure 6.90-2, which three of the following statements are correct? Give yourself a point for answering correctly.

A. Bullish divergence of MACD-Lines

B. Bearish divergence of MACD-Histogram

C. Bearish divergence of MACD-Lines

D. Consider going long, with a stop in the area of 30.25

E. Consider going short, with a stop in the area of 31.65

F. For a trade within the channel, reward-to-risk ratio is better for a long trade

For a bonus point: Identify the chart pattern at point C, at the time of the EMA upturn.

Question 91—A Long Base

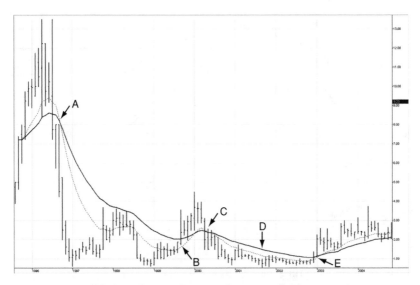

Figure 6.91 Monthly bar chart with 26- and 13-month EMAs.

A monthly chart spanning nine years shows how this stock ran up from $6 to $14 during the 1990s bull market. It collapsed below one dollar in 1997 and has remained in the doghouse ever since, never rising much above $4. The long-term EMA provided sensible guidance even in the multiyear flat zone: Its downturns, A and C, marked the start of bearish phases, and its upturns, B and E, showed where the bulls raised their heads. Which three of the following statements at the right edge of Figure 6.91 are correct?

A. The latest extreme was a new low in 2001; the high of 2004 is below that of 1999—the trend is down.

B. The stock has proven its inability to rise and is not worth monitoring.

C. The expanding monthly ranges since 2003 indicate a growing interest in this stock.

D. A rising EMA indicates an uptrend—go long.

E. Place an order to buy on a monthly closing above $4

For a bonus point: Identify the chart pattern at point D.

Question 92—Prices and Volume

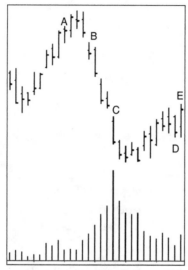

Figure 6.92 Upper pane—daily bar chart. Lower pane—volume.

Cover Figure 6.92 with a sheet of paper and move it slowly from left to right, evaluating each price and volume bar in relation to the previous bars. The date and price markings have been removed to help you focus on the universal features of this chart. You should be able to recognize several fairly common price patterns. Several bars have been marked by letters. Please find each lettered day that corresponds to a number below.

1. A rally confirmed by volume—the bulls win the day

2. A rally unconfirmed by volume

3. A breakaway gap

4. A decline confirmed by volume—the bears win the day

5. An unconfirmed decline

Question 93—Trading Plans and Options

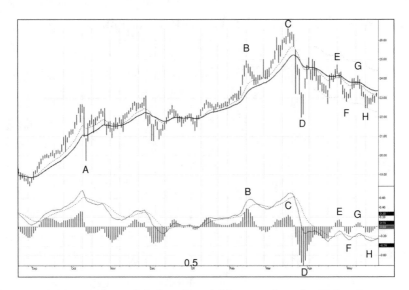

Figure 6.93 Upper pane—daily bar chart with 22- and 13-day EMAs. Lower pane—MACD-Lines and MACD-Histogram 12-26-9.

Figure 6.93 shows a strong upmove in 2004. It accelerated in 2005 but then traced a bearish divergence, B-C. The fall from peak C wiped out in one week what took the bulls four months to achieve. Which four of the following statements are correct?

1. In a downtrend that started at C, pullbacks E and G presented shorting opportunities.

2. A possible alternative to buying a stock is selling a put.

3. A possible alternative to shorting a stock is selling a call.

4. At the right edge of the chart the EMA identifies a downtrend; prices have rallied into a value zone—get ready to short.

5. A bullish divergence D-F-H shows that the downtrend is over—get ready to buy.

For a bonus point: Identify the pattern at point A.

Question 94—Overbought or Oversold

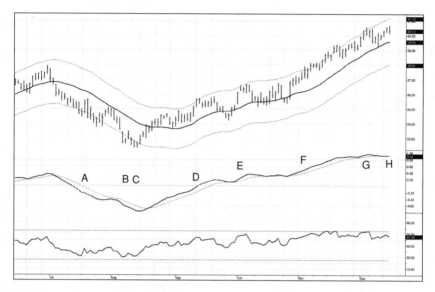

Figure 6.94 Upper pane—daily bar chart with 21-bar SMA and ± 4% envelope. Second pane—MACD-Lines 19-39-9. Bottom pane—14-day RSI.

Figure 6.94 reflects a search for a swing trade. Please identify the following patterns. Give yourself a point for answering correctly.

1. The market is strongly undervalued

2. An actual or potential bullish divergence

3. The market is strongly overvalued

4. An actual or potential bearish divergence

Make a trading decision: At the right edge, does the balance of the evidence favor a long or a short? Explain. Give yourself a point for answering correctly.

TRADERS SPEAK

We are approaching the end of our journey. You have answered questions about different aspects of trading and rated yourself on your knowledge of the markets, trading psychology, tactics, and money management. You have worked through two dozen case studies. Before we part, I want to see how well you remember some of the key statements of traders in *Entries & Exits*.

Once again, I want to acknowledge our debt of gratitude to those who generously opened their trading rooms to us and shared their thoughts, ideas, and findings. Now let us show them that we were paying attention.

Questions	Max. Pts. Available	Trial 1	Trial 2	Trial 3	Trial 4
95	1				
96	1				
97	1				
98	1				
99	1				
100	1				
101	1				
Total points	7				

Question 95—Traders Speak about Organizing Trading

Many traders in *Entries & Exits* commented on how they organize their trading. Which three of the following statements belong to interviewees?

A. Be patient. Be deliberate. Wait for the perfect setup. When you see it, don't hesitate. If it's not happening, don't take action.

B. If you fail to make profits trading stocks, move on to futures and options.

C. Keep a diary, and review it periodically. Write down your thoughts, emotions, and incidents at the time of each trade. You'll be surprised at the valuable information you'll find, particularly about your own behavior patterns.

D. Learning takes a long time. Experience plays a large role.

E. You should approach the market as a blank slate and trade whatever appeals to you after the opening bell.

Question 96—Traders Speak about Psychology

Many traders in *Entries & Exits* commented on trading psychology. Which three of the following statements belong to interviewees?

A. Our goal is to track the crowd and always go against it.

B. Men tend to be more successful traders than women because they can sustain higher losses without becoming emotional.

C. The key question in trading is not "Am I right or am I wrong?" but "Did I apply my methods correctly?"

D. I only trade well when I do not feel excited, elated, or fearful.

E. If you bring normal human habits and tendencies to trading, you'll gravitate toward the majority and inevitably lose.

Question 97—Traders Speak about Money Management

Many traders in *Entries & Exits* commented on money management. Which three of the following statements belong to interviewees?

A. To take a position larger than justified by the capital is to invite disaster.

B. Double up your trade size if a losing position turns around and starts moving in your favor—faster to break even.

C. It is okay to add to a losing position if planned in advance as a part of building a large position.

D. When doubtful, reduce trade size.

Question 98—Traders Speak about Entering Trades

Many traders in *Entries & Exits* commented on entering trades. Which three of the following statements belong to the interviewees?

A. You have to be invested every day; a day without a position is a day lost.

B. Having a written plan for every trade helps avoid impulsive buys and sells.

C. Try not to make too many decisions during the trading day. Plan your trades mostly during non-trading hours.

D. Prices usually begin to move before the fundamental data becomes available—technicals precede fundamentals.

E. It makes little difference whether you enter on open, on close, or intraday.

Question 99—Traders Speak about Exiting Trades

Many traders in *Entries & Exits* commented on exiting trades. Which two of the following statements belong to interviewees?

A. Run quickly or not at all. Run at the first sign of danger, but if you fail to do this, hold on or close out only part of your position.

B. Never discuss closed trades with fellow traders.

C. When a trade goes against you, automatically close out the original position and enter a trade in the opposite direction.

D. If your goal is to make $2,000 from a certain trade, you should not close it out at only $1,900.

E. Have no regrets if the stock you sold continues to rise.

Question 100—Traders Speak about Losses

Many traders in *Entries & Exits* commented on losing money. Which four of the following statements belong to interviewees?

A. I was committed to a bearish outlook and instead of seeing what was happening, I was thinking about what should happen.

B. Intellectually I knew we were at a top.

C. Rely on your intuition to exit a losing trade.

D. There were plenty of clear signals to sit on my hands, but I allowed myself to get sucked into this trade.

E. My mistake was in the poor choice of the stop-loss at the very obvious level just a few ticks below the contract low. I fell into a common trap, and this made my trade the victim of a "fishing expedition" by floor traders.

Question 101—Traders Speak about Trade Management

Many traders in *Entries & Exits* commented on managing trades. Which two of the following statements belong to interviewees?

A. If a stock looks almost perfect but something is missing, walk away and do not beat yourself up if it turns out to be a good trade.

B. If I cannot find any stock that shows my favorite setup, I'll accept an alternative setup.

C. While I always require a perfect setup to trade a stock, I am not as strict in trading futures.

D. Give me this setup a hundred times, and I will take it a hundred times.

E. The brand of toolbox software makes a great difference for traders.

ANSWERS AND RATING SCALES

ORGANIZATION

Answer 1

D.

There is no set amount of time it takes to learn to trade. The outcome depends not only on the material you have to cover but on the changes you have to make in your own personality. The normal human impulse is to run with the crowd, which is deadly in the markets, and some people take longer to unlearn that behavior than others. A steady focus on trading, with specific hours committed to market work, is a good prognostic sign of future success.

Answer 2

C and E.

Trying to make a meaningful amount of money from a tiny account is extremely dangerous. The best course of action is to trade for the track record; a good track record can pull in money from family and friends. A person with a small account must do everything to minimize expenses because they represent a much higher percentage of his account. Looking at options as a cheap substitute for stocks is a dangerous folly—options trade differently from stocks.

Answer 3

Professional—A and E. Serious amateur—B and C. Gambler—D.

In trading, like in any field of human endeavor, professionals make their work a priority, amateurs catch as catch can, and gamblers waltz in when they feel like it. A professional basketball player goes to the gym every day to shoot baskets, a serious amateur joins as many pickup games as he can, and an overweight wannabe steps out into his backyard, throws a ball, and pulls a muscle. A professional in any field makes what he does for a living his first priority—work comes before fun, sometimes before food, occasionally before family. A serious amateur has to earn his living elsewhere, but allocates as much time as he can to the markets. He does his homework in the evenings and on weekends. Someone who looks at the markets only when the mood strikes is clearly a gambler.

Answer 4

3. A and B.

Paper-trading tests your discipline and shows very quickly whether you have the persistence to do your daily homework. Paper-trading to test a new idea for a period of time helps to gauge the effectiveness of your method without risking any money.

Still, there is a deep chasm between a paper trade and real money. When it comes to placing orders, paper-trading gives you flawless executions, but that is not what happens in the real world. A stock you want to sell short comes up as "unable to borrow"; there is sudden massive slippage during a fill; you make a slip of tongue and place a limit order instead of stop-limit order, getting filled at the wrong level. Nor does paper-trading reflect the emotional stress of live trading. It can create unrealistic expectations that are quickly deflated in the rough-and-tumble world of live trading.

Answer 5

4.

A good driver in a Chevy will outrace a beginner in a Ferrari. As an old auto mechanic once said to me, the most important nut in the car is the one behind the wheel. Preoccupation with powerful hardware and the number of screens and other devices often reflects insecurity about one's trading ability. Trading software tends to be undemanding, and even an old computer will do. For me, one of the many attractions of trading is that I can do it on my laptop from almost anywhere in the world.

Answer 6

C and E.

Professional traders may use a variety of tools. Many rely on live data, while others feel perfectly satisfied with the end-of-day charts and do not worry about a delay. At least two traders in *Entries & Exits* rely on manual charting. Not a single one uses a blackbox that gives automatic trading signals—those tend to be popular among beginners who still believe in Santa Claus. While a fax service with both charts and advice may serve as a source of ideas, it can never be the only research tool for a serious trader.

Answer 7

4.

Good record-keeping is essential for successful trading. A serious trader needs to know how to create a spreadsheet to hold his data, check it for accuracy, perform basic calculations, and flash colors when certain conditions are met.

When it comes to Excel, there are two groups of traders at the opposite ends of the spectrum. Computer illiterates are at a huge disadvantage in record-keeping; they would benefit from a basic course or they could hire a tutor to teach them the essential Excel skills. At the other end of the scale, some sophisticated Excel users become so enamored with their software that they spend too much time doing fancy programming instead of focusing on the markets.

Answer 8

E.

A trader without a blackbox is like a fish without a bicycle. Buying such a system and paying someone to trade it for you is the adult equivalent of waiting for Santa. No amount of reduced commissions can compensate for the inherent flaws of this approach.

Answer 9

1–A. 2–A. 3–B. 4–B.

As a rule, it is better to commit more time to the field you know than to look for greener pastures. Analyzing industry groups adds depth and breadth to your homework. Testing your system on a greater number of stocks beats sitting in front of a day-trading monitor. Good records quickly translate into better trading, while adding more timeframes tends to run into the law of diminishing returns. Keeping good records is the main purpose of Excel, while adding more charting packages leads to circling around the same price data.

Answer 10

1–A. 2–B. 3–A. 4–B.

A beginner who allocates a specific amount of money to his education is ahead of the curve. Most people do not allocate nearly enough when they start out and spend way too much after they find themselves in trouble, as if throwing money at a problem could get them out of a mess.

An intelligent trader is generally tight with his money—he keeps expenses in check, concentrates on his education, and stays away from magic solutions, such as commercial tutoring. Going to a conference allows him to meet experts face to face and judge their truthfulness or lack of such, while also networking with other traders.

Answer 11

Useful—A and D.

Most traders are very isolated, giving rise to strange ideas and beliefs that could never withstand the test of being exposed to others for review. It pays to have a trading buddy and a group of people with similar interests; at the same time it is important not to overdo it and spend all your time hanging out in groups. A good measure of the seriousness of your commitment is contributing your work to some like-minded group on a regular basis. It makes no sense to have a group vote on a trade—a camel is a horse designed by a committee.

Answer 12

(Thanks to Michael Brenke on whose interview this question is based.)

True—A, C, and D. False—B and E.

When you start, it would be unreasonable to expect your checklist to be complete from the get-go. As long as your money management is in place, any mistakes will not be deadly, and you will gradually learn to improve your checklist. It will help verify that you follow the essential trading rules, but you have to keep it short and action-oriented, not cluttered by minor details that you may record in your trading diary.

Answer 13

1–B. 2–B. 3–B. 4–A.

Any greenhorn can enter a trade, but it takes knowledge and experience to find a good exit. Risking $100 to make $200 gives a 2:1 reward-to-risk ratio, while risking $500 to make $1,250 improves that to 2.5:1. Any single trade has a fair degree of randomness, and a pro puts his trust in his system, rather than in any individual trade. Spreading your bets to reduce risk on each trade is a sensible tactic.

Grading Your Answers

If a question requires only one answer, you earn a point by answering it correctly. If a question requires several answers (for example, "Which three of the following five statements are correct?"), rate your answer proportionately. If you answer all three correctly, give yourself a point, if two, 0.66, and if only one, 0.33.

11–13: Excellent. You have a good idea of how trading has to be organized. Be sure to implement in practice what you know in theory, and move on to the next chapter.

8–10: Fairly good. You have grasped the basic ideas. Look up the answers to the questions you have missed. Review them and retake this test in a few days.

Below 8: Poor. Do not despair; you are just starting to test yourself. Go back, reread the relevant sections of *Entries & Exits* and *Come into My Trading Room*, then retake this test.

PSYCHOLOGY

Answer 14

(Thanks to Damir Makhmudov, on whose interview this question is based.)

True—A, B, and C.

The more you trade, the faster you'll learn—as long as you keep the size of your trades small and maintain good records. Setting profit targets relatively close to entry levels is useful for beginners. Winners and losers go through personal upswings and downswings; the winners' approach to life helps them learn from their losses and extend winning trends.

Answer 15

(Thanks to Sohail Rabbani, on whose interview this question is based.)

C is not essential.

A serious trader uses money management rules, does not add to losing positions, does not allow a meaningful profit to turn into a loss, and uses protective stops. Having implemented these life-saving rules, he retains a high degree of freedom in his trading choices. Some people like to diversify, while others like to concentrate their holdings. Either method can work, as long as money management is in place.

Answer 16

(Thanks to Mike McMahon, on whose interview this question is based.)

Advantages—A and E. Disadvantages—B, C, and D.

Traders with a scientific background, such as engineers, physicians, and others, bring several useful habits to trading, primarily a facility with numbers and a habit of keeping records. At the same time, their psychological luggage is often counterproductive in the fluid world of trading. The qualities of rigidity and arrogance can be deadly in a rapidly shifting market, where playing the odds is much more appropriate than relying on supposedly certain research findings.

Answer 17

True—A and D.

When an army goes to war, no more than 10% of its troops can be on the firing line, while the rest provide essential support. Good trading must be based on the foundation of solid research and scrupulous record-keeping. As Mike McMahon said in his interview, trading compares to record-keeping like shopping to balancing your checkbook. The more trades you make, the more you can learn—but only if you keep good records and learn from your trades instead of chasing the adrenaline rush. Setting a maximum—or, for that matter, a minimum—number of trades would create an artificial limit. You've got to trade what the market gives you—sometimes a lot and often a little. No system will ever catch all market opportunities, and a dry spell is no reason to chuck a system.

Answer 18

True—B and E.

Certainty exists only in the middle of the chart; it does not live at the right edge. A fruitless search for certainty is the undoing of many educated traders who think they will reach clarity if only they work hard enough. Whenever you enter a trade, you face two risks—a money risk and an information risk. The pros are comfortable with uncertainty, as long as their financial risk is low. Beginners, on the other hand, keep waiting for more confirmations and end up risking a lot more money.

Answer 19

D.

Many incoming e-mails reflect passivity and laziness. Asking about free data is easier than typing the same question into Google. Asking for indicator settings reflects unwillingness to do independent research. Asking another person what trading methods to use is an attempt to take a huge shortcut, while throwing one's family into that question lays a guilt trip on the recipient. All the commercial "mentors" I've ever seen looked very sharky, preying on the weakest traders. If you are lucky to find a mentor, it will not be through an ad. Good relationships involve a high degree of reciprocity. The trader who asks you to look at his work has obviously done his own research. It is always interesting to see how another person's mind works.

Answer 20

True—D, E, and F.

Trading is a private activity, and it is best not to discuss your planned or actual trades with others, to avoid being influenced by them. Once you close out a trade, it might be a good idea to share its lessons with trusted friends. Duplicating a position is not a good idea because you're likely to be left holding the bag after your tipper exits that trade. The only sensible use of tips is as an intelligence-gathering system—record the source of each tip and drop it into your system to test whether it fits in with your method.

Answer 21

(Thanks to Gerald Appel, on whose interview this question is based.)

True—A and D.

Financial markets have several advantages over non-financial games. Transaction costs are lower (a track may take 20% or more from every bet). You can enter and exit throughout market hours, in effect betting after the start of the race and cashing out before the end. A professional player who knows how to manage money has an advantage, and many traders have gambled at some point. Following Lady Luck and looking for excitement is the undoing of traders and gamblers alike.

Answer 22

(Thanks to Peter Tatarnikov, on whose interview this question is based.)

True—A and E.

Professionals sometimes say that the market is three-quarters psychology and one-quarter economics. Beginners, driven by greed and fear, tend to grab profits too quickly but hang on to losses for too long. Frightened people like to huddle; they place stops at obvious levels, allowing the pros to hit them. When the crowd reaches a high degree of consensus, it means that the mass of small traders is on the one side of the markets, while a smaller, richer group is on the opposite side, making a reversal more likely.

Answer 23

True—B and E.

The crowd is suspicious of new trends, gradually warms up to them, and jumps in with both feet toward the end of a move. When company news make the front page, it is usually pretty stale and the trend is near its final stage. "Nobody ever went broke underestimating the intelligence of a crowd," wrote P. T. Barnum, a famous American entrepreneur, more than a century ago. The media reflects crowd opinions, and when it becomes very one-sided, the market is usually ready to reverse.

Answer 24

Likely—A, B, and D. Unlikely—C and E.

Losers often suffer from indecision and self-doubt. Many imagine that a bigger account would allow them to trade better. This is a fantasy— I have seen traders wipe out accounts of more than a hundred million dollars. When self-control is lax, account size does not matter. Losers do not like to perform useful but unexciting and time-consuming tasks, such as keeping good records or scrupulously applying money management rules.

Answer 25

True—B and E.

Inexperienced traders tend to pull the trigger with great confidence— a trader becomes fearful only after he has traded for a while and received a serious beating from the market. In order to regain confidence it is best to trade a tiny size and only gradually increase it as the fear recedes; willpower alone is not enough, and good trading ideas do not reduce fear.

Answer 26

C—E—A.

The first step for a traumatized trader is to pause for a while—this lets him heal and plan. Allocating a specific block of time to the market reflects a commitment to reform. So do record-keeping and money management. When this trader returns to the market, he should start moving forward in tiny steps; trading a tiny size will reduce the pressure to perform. Being super-critical or shifting to new markets is useless. There are winners in all markets, while others keep losing because of their own unresolved problems.

Grading Your Answers

If a question requires only one answer, you earn a point by answering it correctly. If a question requires several answers (for example, "Which two of the following five statements are correct?"), rate your answer proportionately. If you find both answers, give yourself a point, but if only one, then half a point.

11–13: Excellent. You are well aware of the psychological factors in trading. Be sure to keep notes on your feelings about entering and exiting trades in your trading diary.

8–10: Fairly good. You have some grasp of the importance of trading psychology, but this is too important a topic to settle for anything less than excellent. Look up the answers to the questions you've missed, review them, and retake the test in a few days.

Below 8: Poor. Now is the time to stop, return to the books, and reread the relevant sections of *Entries & Exits*, *Come into My Trading Room*, and other books on trading psychology recommended by the interviewees.

MARKETS

Answer 27

B, C, and E.

A tick is the smallest price change allowed in any given market. Since different markets are priced differently, their ticks differ from one another. For example, a tick in most U.S. stocks is a penny, but very low-priced stocks move in even smaller increments. A tick in e-minis is 0.25 cents but it is 0.10 cents in a full S&P contract, while a tick in grains is still measured the old-fashioned way—in eighths.

Answer 28

E.

As Anna Akhmatova wrote in one of her poems, "If only you knew amidst what trash flowers grow, feeling no shame." You can find your picks anywhere—including such trashy sources as tips at a drunken party—as long as you put them through a rigorous filtering process of your analytic and trading system. A serious trader does not trade tips—he uses them as fodder for his own research.

Answer 29

D and E.

Interest rates and bonds are at the opposite ends of a see-saw—when one end is up, the other must be down. Rising interest rates mean falling bond prices and vice versa.

Answer 30

A or B.

While prices of all trading vehicles are measured in dollars or other currencies, the prices of currencies are measured against one other. When the U.S. dollar drops sharply, other currencies, such as the euro and the yen, must rise. Some may rise more and others less, but the direction of their change has to be contrary to that of the dollar.

Answer 31

D.
Bonus question: False.

Stock industry groups and subgroups combine large numbers of stocks in related fields. A trader can find a group or a subgroup and look for the most promising stocks in it according to his criteria. Different organizations classify stocks differently. For example, at the time of this writing there are 197 groups in the Investor's Business Daily list, but 239 groups and subgroups in the Telechart list.

Answer 32

3—C and D are incorrect.

It is possible to review approximately 200 stock industry groups in a couple of hours and gain a broad overview of the entire stock market. If you try to spend just 10 seconds analyzing each of 10,000 stocks, that project would take more than 24 hours.

Industry group analysis paints a more precise picture of the entire market than the broad indexes, such as the S&P500. Groups often show signs of emerging strength or weakness in advance of the broad indexes. The only way to identify such changes is by analyzing groups on a regular weekly basis.

Answer 33

C.

It is a good idea to start with the general and work your way down to the specific. Analyzing groups helps you discover the strongest and the weakest areas of the stock market. Look for buy candidates among the strongest stocks in the strongest groups and shorting candidates among the weakest stocks in the weakest groups.

Answer 34

Long stock—A or D. Short stock—B or C.

A bull may buy a stock, buy a call, or write a put. In the long run, buying calls is the most dangerous of these methods. A stock owner may sit on his position until it does what he expects, but a call buyer is running against the clock. He may win a lap or two in this race but is sure to lose in the long run. The time works for the put writer, but he has another source of stress—being subject to a potentially unlimited loss makes most people jumpy and they get easily shaken out of their positions. Professionals manage stress by properly sizing their positions and being prepared to act whenever a trade goes against them.

Answer 35

2—B and C are incorrect.

Closing your eyes to any area of market research can be dangerous. The profitability of gold producers depends on whether the price of gold is above or below their production cost. Volatility soars as the price of gold approaches that line. Stocks can triple and quadruple, which rarely happens with metal prices. Commodities only seem more volatile because they can be traded on razor-thin margins.

Answer 36

Futures—D. Options—E. Both—B and C. Neither—A.

Futures and options are derivatives, dependent on the price of another product, such as a stock or a commodity. Their lifetime is limited to a few months, although occasionally it can be more than a year. Normally, the more time left to the expiration, the more expensive futures and options. In a bull market caused by a shortage of a commodity, its nearby months can become more expensive than faraway months, resulting in a so-called inverted market. You can walk away from an option, but you have to buy your way out of a losing futures trade; this scares away beginners but leads to more favorable pricing. Higher reward with lower risk is an advertising slogan, as real as a visit from Santa.

Answer 37

3.

The more you know about the market you're trading, the better off you're likely to be. It is essential to know that a penny move in corn will swing your account up or down $50 per contract, but that same penny will translate into $375 per contract in coffee. Only a rank beginner will call his broker with an order to buy cocoa at noon, only to be told this market is already closed. Missing the first notice day can cost you money because you might have to wiggle out from under an exercise notice. At the same time, there is no need to overdo information gathering. The previous contracts are closed and gone, you're trading the current one, and that's the one whose data you must keep current.

Answer 38

True—A and D.

There is no perfect answer to the problem of analyzing long-term futures prices with their gaps at the time of rollover. Trying to splice together two disparate price series on the same chart is fraught with complications. The practical answer is to analyze two data series for each future. Use a perpetual contract for long-term analysis, but zoom in on the latest contract for precision timing of the specific contract you will be trading.

Grading Your Answers

If a question requires only one answer, you earn a point by answering it correctly. If a question requires several answers (for example, "Which three of the following five statements are correct?"), rate your answer proportionately. If you find all three, give yourself a point, if two, 0.66, and if only one, 0.33.

The grading of this section is a little more permissive than that of the previous ones. If you do not plan to trade futures or options, you do not need to know every little detail about them. Still, the markets are interconnected, and a serious trader in any market should have a basic familiarity with other fields.

10–13: Excellent. You have the key facts at your fingertips. Be sure to keep abreast of any changes in the markets you are trading.

7–9: Fairly good. You know quite a bit about the markets, but still have gaps to fill. Most brokers provide informative brochures with specific facts. Look up the answers to the questions you've missed, review them, and retake the test in a few days.

Below 7: Poor. The fact that you answered less than half the questions correctly means that you are stumbling in the dark. You have no business putting a single dollar at risk until you fill the gaps in your knowledge. *How to Buy Stocks* by Engel should help beginning stock traders, *The Futures Game* by Teweles & Jones—futures traders, and *Options as a Strategic Investment* by McMillan—options traders.

TRADING TACTICS

Answer 39

A, B, or E.

There is a great deal of noise in the financial markets. Doing your homework on a weekend and making decisions while the markets are closed helps reduce their emotional push and pull. You have to treat your own decision-making process with respect. You certainly would not discard your analysis and decisions because of the news; you may want to become a little more cautious, depending on the source of the news.

Answer 40

A.

A major difference between professionals and amateurs is that the pros expect to make money in the long run. They know that any single trade has a high degree of randomness, and trust their system more than any individual pick. Amateurs become unnerved by a few losing trades. Do not change your horses while fording the river—you made your plan before entering the trade. You own both the trade and the plan—stick with them!

Answer 41

2—A and B.

Following your trading plan is a rational choice. Still, it might make sense to exit a market that starts behaving in an unexpected manner and reevaluate it from the sidelines. It rarely pays to complicate an already tense situation by throwing in more indicators and timeframes, further increasing the confusion.

Answer 42

True—A and E.

Volatility tends to rise around the time of earnings reports—this is a fact that no serious trader can afford to ignore. Stocks can react to earnings in unexpected ways, often falling after good earnings are released. Because of this volatility and uncertainty, it is best to avoid trading stocks at earnings time. Still, if you get a very strong signal, follow it! It may well reflect the behavior of insiders buying or selling ahead of the news.

Answer 43

True—A, B, and E.

You can expect volatility to jump when people feel afraid and normal supply-demand relationships are disrupted. An experienced sailor reefs his sails during a storm, and an experienced trader reduces his position size during a hurricane in the financial markets. You may feel tempted to increase your size to take advantage of a windfall, but heightened volatility should make you even more mindful of risk control. Stocks can go down or up, commodities can gyrate, but the government can be expected to have a knee-jerk reaction to a disaster—it usually floods the system with liquidity to soften the blow, which drives down interest rates and lifts bond prices, at least in the short run.

Answer 44

(Thanks to Andrea Perolo, on whose interview this question is based.)

True—B, C, and E.

Classical charting keeps you closer to price data than technical indicators, whose key advantage is objectivity. Putting a ruler on a chart is a somewhat subjective exercise. No method is perfect, and what looks like a trendline break may well turn out to be a false break before the trend resumes. A serious analyst may prefer classical charting or computerized analysis, but he'll never be an extremist. For example, Andrea is primarily a classical chartist, but he also uses technical indicators and such tools as seasonality and Commitments of Traders reports.

Answer 45

(Thanks to David Weis, on whose interview this question is based.)

Likely continuation—B and D. Likely reversal—A and C.

A tall bar during a rally, closing near the high, indicates that bulls won the day; their strength is likely to carry over into tomorrow's opening. A downside breakout with high volume on a high-range day shows that bears were strong and are likely to press their advantage tomorrow. A tall bar during a rally, followed by a short and stunted bar, shows that the trend is running into resistance. A narrow-range day with high volume shows a lot of effort for a minimal gain—a sign of resistance to the ongoing trend.

Answer 46

B and C are acceptable.

There are so many trading opportunities that you do not need to chase any one of them. If you are confident about your skills, you know there will always be another good trade coming soon. A gap opening puts the stock closer to your profit target and farther away from the stop, shifting the risk-reward balance. If you are super-bullish on that stock and still want to buy it, you need to recalculate permitted trade size. It is probably not a good idea to leave an order in place at the originally planned level—just imagine how the chart will look if that order gets filled. It will show an upside gap followed by a retracement back into the range—a bearish pattern. Deleting a stock that disappointed you from the list and never looking at it again would be amateurish. The more you know about a stock, the better prepared you'll be to trade it in the future.

Answer 47

(Thanks to Gerald Appel, on whose interview this question is based.)

  True—A, B, and C.

Trends attract our attention, but the markets spend most of their time going nowhere. Uptrends favor bulls and downtrends bears, but trading ranges have a way of chewing up both sides. If you correctly identify a trend, even a trade with a sloppy entry and exit can end up being profitable, but there is no such luxury in non-trending markets—they require much greater precision.

Answer 48

(Thanks to Kerry Lovvorn, on whose interview this question is based.)

  True—C and D.

Just as uptrends alternate with downtrends, stocks go through periods of higher and lower volatility. Entering during a period of low volatility and exiting when volatility rises allows you to profit from those transitions. The "squeeze play" described by Kerry in his interview offers a good example of profiting from a change in volatility.

Answer 49

(Thanks to Bill Doane, on whose interview this question is based.)

True—B and C.

The bigger the foundation, the taller the building—great uptrends tend to emerge from multi-year trading ranges. Major bull and bear markets are linked to economic cycles, which is why the stocks in the same industry tend to emerge either early or late in a bull market—Bill calls this tendency "recycling." A pullback into the base following what looked like a major breakout is a sign of danger—a rocket is not supposed to sink back onto its launching pad. When you try to catch a major trend, it is important to let your profits run, but just as important to cut your losses short.

Answer 50

A, B, and D.

An EMA tends to go flat when prices become locked in a tight trading range; when it turns up, it confirms an uptrend. Buying a pullback to a rising EMA or selling short a rally towards a falling EMA means trading at value. The zone between a fast and a slow EMA helps identify the value zone for that trading vehicle. The signals of the longer EMAs are more reliable than those of the short EMAs, but they take longer to develop. This is why it pays to use a combination of a fast and a slow EMA on the same chart. Prices rallying to a record distance from an EMA could be either a sign of strength or a terminal splash of bullishness as the uptrend tops out.

Answer 51

D.

A moving average represents an average consensus of value; it has a lot more inertia than price. The price can change by a wide margin from day to day, but a moving average tends to chug along at a steady pace. For example, if it has been rising by 20 cents a day for the past few days, you can reasonably expect it to rise another 20 cents tomorrow. Adding 20 cents to the day's closing EMA value shows you where that EMA is likely to be tomorrow.

Answer 52

(Thanks to Ray Testa, Jr., on whose interview this question is based.)

True—C, D, and E.

Amateurs tend to buy upside breakouts and short downside breakouts, looking for an elusive major trend to make them a lot of money in a hurry. Professionals know that most breakouts are false, and tend to use channel walls as targets for profit-taking. When prices hit a channel while indicators show a divergence, they provide an especially strong warning of an impending reversal. Using channel height to rate your trades links your performance to the potential profit available in that market.

Answer 53

First order—B, C, and E. Second order—A and D. Bonus—Weekly.

Technical analysis is partly science and partly art; answers to these questions are somewhat subjective. I am sure that some professional traders would answer them differently. The longer the timeframe, the more important its signals; a pattern on the weekly chart carries more weight than the same pattern on the dailies.

Answer 54

B.

The Impulse system is a censorship system—it tells you when you are allowed to enter a trade. It is very permissive with the exits, but like any system, it must be underpinned with an iron discipline of loss control. You have no business waiting until the 2% Rule is violated—you must get out before that happens.

Answer 55

(Thanks to Fred Schutzman, on whose interview this question is based.)

3—5—1—2—4.

A common error in system development is a mindless mining of historical data for patterns that had been profitable in the past. A pattern not based on some logical concept of market behavior is highly unlikely to persist. If you start out with a concept of market behavior that makes sense, then all subsequent steps logically flow from it. You can express the rules, eyeball the signals on the charts, test them rigorously with a computer, evaluate the results, make adjustments, and so on. As Fred wrote in his e-mail, "With lots of hard work and dedication, anyone can build a successful trading system. It is not easy, but it is certainly within reach. As with most things in life, what you get out of this effort will be directly related to what you put into it."

Answer 56

(Thanks to Fred Schutzman, on whose interview this question is based.)

True—A, C, and D.

Once you begin trading a mechanical system, you have to take all of its signals, otherwise you stop being a system trader and become a discretionary trader. Your system should be based on some logical concept of how markets behave rather than curve-fitting past data. You must focus on the system as a whole, not on any individual trade. Still, you would not want to follow a system to the edge of a cliff and into the abyss—a good system will include signals that tell you when it stops working and should be suspended.

Needless to say, these rules have to be put in place before you start and not as an afterthought. Do not discard the system that stopped working—it may yet become profitable again when markets change. Nothing is guaranteed in the future except for change.

Answer 57

(Thanks to Dr. Diane Buffalin, on whose interview this question is based.)

True—B, D, or E.

"Selling a put is no more risky than buying a stock," said Diane during our interview, "as long as I do not freeze if it goes against me." Selling a naked put, which becomes less valuable as the stock rises, is a bet that the stock will rise or stay flat. If that stock begins to slide, a naked put writer is in danger—there is no profit to count, only a deepening loss. Buying a stock under those circumstances would only compound the stress. One course of action would be to buy the put back; others would be to sell a call or short the stock.

Answer 58

A—2. B—1. C—5. D—3. E—4.

Many analysts and traders know that volume moves prices. Most volume-based indicators take the entire day's volume as a whole. Pascal created a method for slicing each day's prices and volume into one-minute segments and isolating volume that led to price changes. Small Effective Volume reflects the behavior of public traders, while Large Effective Volume helps find the footprints of institutions that often dominate the markets.

Grading Your Answers

If a question requires only one answer, you earn a point by answering it correctly. If a question requires several answers (for example, "Which two of the following five statements are correct?"), rate your answer proportionately. If you find both answers, give yourself a point, but if only one, then half a point.

You do not have to earn a perfect score in this section if you do not use all of the methods described here. Still, a competent trader is familiar with the main methods used by his competitors. This knowledge helps him anticipate how the market crowd will move in response to this or that change in the market.

17–21: Excellent. You have a good grasp of key trading tactics. Now is the time to focus on money management and record-keeping.

12–16: Fairly good. You are operating above the newcomer level, but this area is too important to settle for anything less than excellent performance. Look up the answers to the questions you've missed, review them, and retake the test in a few days.

Below 12: Poor. Missing more than half the questions on market tactics should sound a loud warning signal. Professional traders are waiting for you in the markets, ready to take your money. Before you do battle with them, you must bring yourself up to speed in trading tactics. Please review the techniques described in *Entries & Exits* and then retake this test.

MONEY MANAGEMENT AND RECORD-KEEPING

Answer 59

B.

The worst thing to happen to a newbie who expects his stock to go to the moon is to win. Assured of his brilliance, he loads up on the next great idea, goes on margin—and loses all his profits plus a big chunk of his starting capital. The 2% Rule is designed to prevent such disasters. Two percent of $74,000 comes to $1,480—this is the maximum permitted risk per trade. Buying at $7 with a stop at $5.60 means risking $1.40 per share. Dividing total permitted risk by risk per share shows that he is allowed to buy 1,000 shares, with a few dollars left over to cover commissions and possibly slippage.

Answer 60

A, C, and D.

The 2% Rule sets the maximum level of risk per trade for any account. You cannot risk more but are perfectly welcome to risk less. If you risk 2% on every trade, the 6% Rule will limit you to only three trades. Many traders like to risk less than 2% per trade and carry more positions. A trader recovering from a bad loss or testing a new idea may choose to trade a tiny size, such as 100 shares. Only a gambler would not count his risk on a margin loan.

Answer 61

D.

The 6% Rule allows a trader to risk no more than 6% of his account equity in any given month. This means that the total permitted risk in a $74,000 account is $4,440. This trader's first three trades of the month are now risk-free, with stops at breakeven levels. His other three open trades, with $1,200 risk in each, put a total of $3,600 at risk, leaving $840 of available risk. He has to reduce the size of the planned trade to fit into his total available risk of $4,440 per month. He may also reduce or close out one of the three positions where he still has money at risk. This would allow him to free up more available risk and trade up the full 1,000 shares in his newly planned trade.

Answer 62

No.

The 6% Rule limits the total risk for the month for this account to 6% of $52,000, or $3,120. The first trade was a breakeven, no longer counted against the risk. The two losing trades ate up $1,500 of permitted risk capital, leaving the trader with only $1,620 of available risk for the rest of that month. The two open trades put $1,300 of that amount at risk, leaving only $320 of available risk. This trader has to reduce the size of his planned trade or close out one of his open positions in order to free up risk capital for a more attractive trade.

Answer 63

Legal: B, D, and E.
Illegal: A, C, and F.

It is easy to find how many shares you may trade using the 2% Rule. Calculate 2% of your account; calculate the distance from your entry point to your stop to find your risk per share; and divide the first by the second to find the maximum number of shares the Rule allows you to buy.

Answer 64

4—A, B, C, and D are correct.

You need to record the date, price, and size of every trade. Serious traders keep scrupulous records of trading-related expenses. The necessity of keeping commission level down is widely understood, but most traders are shocked after they start keeping track of their slippage. For most people, slippage vastly exceeds commission level; you need to record the level at which you wanted to trade as well as the level at which you got filled. At the same time, a spreadsheet should be streamlined and not cluttered with only tangentially relevant data.

Answer 65

B and C are correct.

People who do not learn from the past are doomed to repeat their errors. A diary makes you look at your past actions and learn from them. It inserts an educational loop into the trading process. Your feelings are at least as important to your success or failure as technical signals. You can usually learn more from losing trades than from winning ones.

Answer 66

B and D are correct.

Rating your trades helps concentrate on improving performance. A total profit or loss is a crude measure that depends to a large extent on the market you are trading and your trade size. A more refined measure of performance is the percentage of the trading channel captured during each trade. It is not dependent on the market or the trade size but reflects your finesse in capturing the swing of the market within its channel. Mike McMahon and Damir Makhmudov in *Entries & Exits* showed you how they use that measure, and several other traders in the book use it in their work.

It is surprisingly hard to buy in the lower half of a day's bar and sell in the upper half. To enter or exit a trade you must run through a shallow pool of piranhas—day-traders who make their money on intraday fluctuations. Keeping track of the quality of your entries and exits provides a useful measure of your level of trading skills. At the same time, one should not get distracted by the extraneous data. Watching the best performing stock in the market is like watching a movie star but neglecting your own life.

Answer 67

1—profit $1.50, channel $6. Captured 25%—rated B.
2—loss $1.50 —rated D.
3—profit $6, channel $18. Captured 33%—rated A.
4—profit $1, channel $8. Captured 12%—rated C.

Prices swing between the upper and the lower channel boundaries and occasionally overshoot them. Comparing your profit in each trade to the height of that stock's daily channel allows you to see what percentage of the swing's potential you have captured.

Answer 68

4—All are correct.

Human memory is imperfect, and traders often forget to trade repetitive market patterns. If you separate your market research into several important segments—indexes, groups, individual stocks—and record your ratings, you will be ahead of the market crowd. It pays to chart those ratings along with key market indexes. Major fundamental developments, such as Fed announcements or releases of key national statistics, often push the stock market up or down. Stocks tend to be more volatile around the time of earnings releases.

Answer 69

Acceptable—A, B, and D.

Safety before profits—place a stop before a "take profit" order. Also, if your broker does not accept OCO orders, perhaps it is time to look for another who does. Using limit orders helps avoid slippage, a major hidden cost in trading. Switching from a limit to a market order when a stock begins to run is amateurish. Do not rely on your memory when placing orders. Many traders have an embarrassing experience of placing a buy instead of a sell when entering orders from memory in a hurry.

Grading Your Answers

If a question requires only one answer, you earn a point by answering it correctly. If a question requires several answers (for example, "Which three of the following five statements are correct?"), rate your answer proportionately. If you find all three, give yourself a point, if two, 0.66, and if only one, 0.33.

There can be nothing permissive about the grading of this section. Mind, Method, and Money are the three M's of successful trading, but unfortunately, money management is the weakest area for the majority of traders. The quality of your trading records has a greater impact on your success or failure than any technical tool or indicator, but most people keep very poor records. If this chapter forces you to focus on these key areas of trading, I will know that creating this book has served a purpose.

10–11: Excellent. You are one of the rare individuals who know the importance of money management and record-keeping. You are ready to proceed to case studies in the next section.

8–9: Fairly good. You have a basic grasp of key concepts of money management and record-keeping—but the topic is too important to accept anything less than a perfect score. Please look up the answers to the questions you've missed, review them, and retake the test in a few days.

Below 8: Poor. The fact that you missed more than a third of the answers in this chapter shows that you are skating on very thin ice. Before you go a step further, stop and review the appropriate sections in *Entries & Exits* and *Come into My Trading Room*. Keep retaking this test until you earn an excellent score and implement everything you learned in your own money management and record-keeping.

CASE STUDIES

Answer 70

Group 1—A, D, and H. Group 2—B, C, E, F, and G. *Bonus:* F.

Exponential moving averages (EMAs) help identify trends, especially on the weekly charts. The rising slope of an EMA reflects growing bullishness, and a declining slope reflects increasing bearishness. When the slope changes direction, it marks a shift of the trend. When the 26-week EMA of CHTR turned up in the spring 2003 (A), it marked the start of a bull market that lasted for over a year, until that EMA turned down in spring 2004 (D); a recent upturn in the summer of 2005 is calling for an end of the bear market (H).

In addition, a moving average helps differentiate between value trades and "greater fool theory" trades. Pullbacks into the value zone between 26-week and 13-week EMAs (B and C) marked good buying opportunities during the bull market. Pullbacks into the value zone during a bear market (E, F, and G) identified shorting opportunities, although shorting such a cheap stock may not have been a good idea.

At point F, in the summer of 2004, a brief rally into the value zone suddenly gathered steam. Prices shot above both EMAs, only to collapse back into their tight weave, and the downtrend resumed. Such fingers, or kangaroo tails, sticking out of congestion zones, help identify important reversal points.

Answer 71

A, D, and E. *Bonus:* A bullish upturn of the EMA.

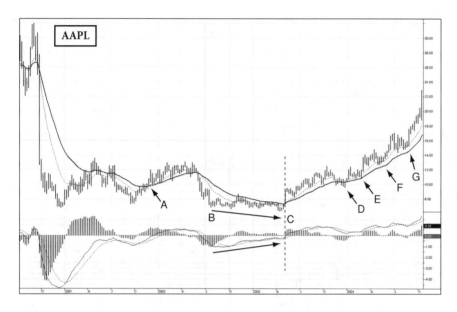

Figure 6.71A

A divergence between MACD-Histogram and price is perhaps the strongest signal in technical analysis; when MACD-Lines also diverge, the signal is even stronger (B—C). But this is not all! Just prior to these dual bullish divergences, AAPL broke down to a new low, but instead of following through to the downside, it reversed, pulled back above the previous low, and rallied above its EMA, leaving behind a false downside breakout. This combination of bullish technical signals amidst fundamental gloom and doom provided a forceful message to buy.

The good fundamental news came later. All those people with iPods you see on the streets swung Apple's balance sheets heavily to the plus side and pushed its stock to 48 before it paused. A rising EMA nicely framed the bullish move, with pullbacks at D, E, F, and G signaling great buying opportunities.

Answer 72

A, B, C, and E. *Bonus:* A weakening of Force Index.

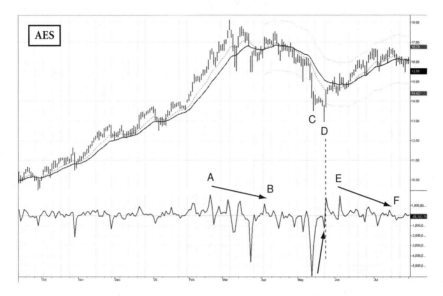

Figure 6.72A

The message of a downward spike of Force Index is different from that of an upward spike. A stock can keep going higher even after several upward spikes, but a forceful downward spike indicates panic, which usually marks at least a minor bottom and sometimes an upside reversal. It shows that the weakest holders have been flushed out, and the stock is ready to go up. A bullish message of the downward spike at point D is reinforced by a bullish divergence (C-D) and the fact that the downside breakout of AES was immediately followed by a reversal and a rally above the latest minor trading range.

Of course, you would not buy AES at D without first looking at the weekly chart. Had you decided to go long, putting a stop at 13 would have given too much leeway to bulls. In trying to catch a quick reversal, the rule should be "Put up or shut up." Placing a stop at level C would have been perfectly sufficient, while saving 50 cents of risk per share.

The multi-week weakening of Force Index A-B (punctuated by a spike and a quick rally) helped identify the important top in March and April. A divergence, E-F, near the right edge of Figure 6.72A indicates that all is not well with AES: Watch out below!

Answer 73

(Thanks to Ray Testa, Jr., on whose actual trade this question is based.)

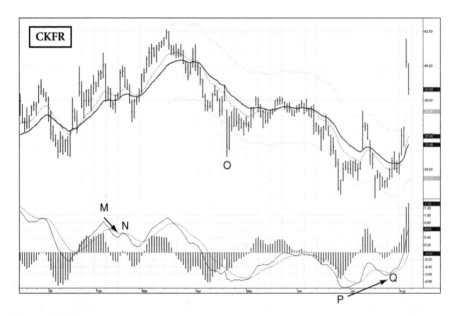

Figure 6.73A

Weekly chart (Figure 6.73-1): 1—A, C, and E. 2—B, D, and F. True—3, 4, and 5.

Daily chart (Figure 6.73-2): 1—P-Q. 2—O. 3—M-N. 5 is correct.

The Impulse system is based on two indicators: the slope of the EMA, which shows market inertia, and the slope of MACD-Histogram, which reflects the push of the dominant market crowd. When these two indicators contradict one another, the Impulse turns neutral, allowing you to either buy, sell short, or stand aside.

While the weekly Impulse is neutral, the daily chart is a screaming buy. A bullish divergence of MACD-Histogram, perhaps the strongest signal in technical analysis, has just given a buy signal, P-Q. It is reinforced by a spiky-looking false break to a new low at Q. With this combination of signals telling us to buy CKFR and the weekly neutral, you need to go long.

Answer 74

(Thanks to Michael Brenke on whose actual trade this question is based.)

A—Down. B—Decreasing. C—Two. D—Long.

The slope of the moving average identifies a downtrend. The narrowing Bollinger bands identify falling volatility. MACD-Histogram and Momentum show bullish divergences, while Stochastic is in gear with the downtrend.

At the next-to-last bar BRCM broke below its early morning low by two cents. There the downtrend stalled, while volatility fell and two out of three oscillators showed bullish divergences. The market appeared ready for an upside reversal.

Figure 6.74A

Day-trading is a tough game. Mike bought near the lower Bollinger band, held for about a half-hour, and sold as soon as the rally ran into resistance. The five-minute bar during which he sold was very narrow, indicating a lack of progress, while the indicators rose toward oversold levels. This sort of trading requires a very high degree of concentration and flawless reflexes.

Answer 75

(Thanks to Damir Makhmudov on whose actual trade this question is based.)

Weekly chart (Figure 6.75-1): 1—D. 2—A. 3—B-C. 4, 5, and 6 are all correct.

Daily chart (Figure 6.75-2): 1—M and O. 2—N. 3—P-S. 4—Q and R. 5 and 7 are correct.

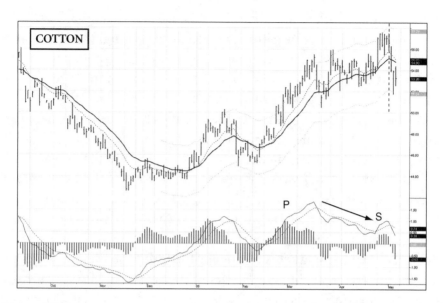

Figure 6.75A

Professional traders like to trade against extremes. Falling MACD-Histogram on both weekly and daily charts indicates that bulls are becoming weaker. Prices in both timeframes are high above their EMAs, indicating overbought conditions. When the weekly Impulse is blue, based on a rising EMA and falling MACD, a trader may take his clues solely from the daily charts. Damir shorted above value and covered after cotton fell below value and its decline appeared to have stalled.

Answer 76

(Thanks to Andrea Perolo on whose actual trade this question is based.)

Weekly chart (Figure 6.76-1): 1—C-D. 2—A-B. 3—B and D. 4—B, F, and H. 5—D, E, and G.

Daily chart (Figure 6.76-2): 1—P-R. 2—M-O. 3—N, R, and T. 4—O, Q, and U. 5—N, P, R, T, and V.

Decision—Short.

The questions to ask yourself at the right edge of any chart are whether that chart is bullish or bearish and whether to go long, short, or stand aside. *Entries & Exits* showed that traders can make money with different and even contradictory approaches, as long as they are consistent and use proper money management.

At the right edge of both weekly and daily charts, wheat is near the upper edge of its narrowing trading range, an oversold area. Still, MACD-Histogram is rising on both weekly and daily charts—and the Impulse system trader would want to see the slope of the EMA before making any decision. Andrea, who is more of a classical chartist, saw this situation differently. He wrote: "Weekly MACD-H is showing nice weakness of the bulls while the market is approaching its trendline. On the daily chart the market is testing for the fifth time the upper trendline of the triangle, showing a triple divergence of MACD-H. Also important to consider is that the seasonal pattern for September wheat strongly suggests a temporary high around mid-July, with at least three weeks' slide."

Figure 6.76A

Andrea used trendlines, resistance, seasonals, and MACD-Histogram to find an oversold level in wheat and sell it short. The trade worked out well—wheat fell below its trendline. When the decline stalled and prices began to bounce, it was time to cover shorts.

Answer 77

(Thanks to Gerald Appel for suggesting this question.)

1—A-B. 2—D-E. 3—C, D, and E. 4—A wedge. *Bonus:* Long.

All traders watch prices, but only the pros pay attention to time. Before he put on this trade, Gerald Appel identified a one-month cycle in the NASDAQ—up one month, down the next. This made him aware that at the right edge of the chart time was running out on the downtrend. Prices fell out of their channel, creating an extremely oversold area, while RSI traced bullish divergence. A falling wedge reflects a slow

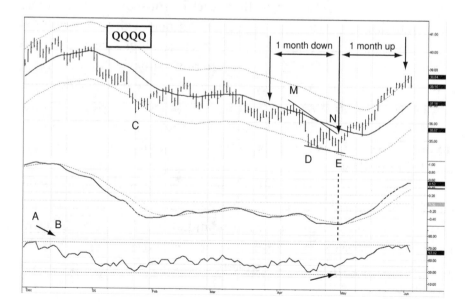

Figure 6.77A

grind to the downside, often followed by an explosive upmove. The risk-reward ratio was good, with just a short distance to the stop below the low, E, and a long way to the profit target at the upper channel line.

The trade worked out well, sending QQQQ into a powerful rally. The bottom, D-E, in Figure 6.77, with its bullish divergences and a declining wedge, looks clear in retrospect. A professional trader identifies a pattern early in the game and does not always wait for every piece of information to fall into place, the way a beginner must do.

Answer 78

(Thanks to Mike McMahon who provided his actual trade for this question.)

True—Weekly (Figure 6.78-1) 1, 2, 3, and 5; Daily (Figure 6.78-2) 6, 8, and 10.

The weekly chart shows that WY ran into stiff resistance near $68 in 2002. Whenever it returned to that level in subsequent years, there were bearish divergences. False breakouts to new highs are very bearish. Mike wrote: "I was scanning for 52-week new highs which I wanted to short and new lows which I wanted to buy. I quickly discovered that it was of little use to look at new highs/lows on the day they occurred since there was no time for them to reverse. So I developed several scans to look for new highs and lows in previous months. WY showed up on my 'New Highs two months back' scan and, after reviewing it, I decided to trade it."

The "new high" refers to spike G on the weekly and U on the daily chart (where it is more visible). Daily MACD-Histogram shows the weakness of bulls for the past month, and at the right edge the EMA turns down as bears gain control. Mike covered his shorts after the stock gapped down, creating a wide bar but closing well off its lows—a clean, professional exit.

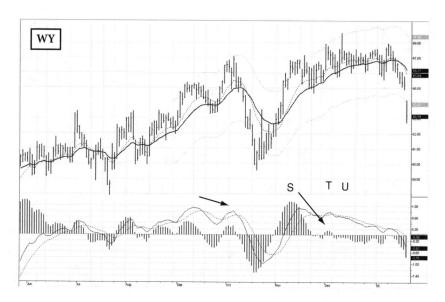

Figure 6.78A

Answer 79

(Thanks to Kerry Lovvorn who provided his actual trade for this question.)

1—B-D and G-H. 2—A-B and E-F. 3—C-D and F-H. 6 is correct.

Standard deviation channels, also called Bollinger bands, expand and contract in response to changes in volatility. While a regular envelope maintains a constant width, these bands squeeze prices when the volatility falls and fly far apart when it rises. Just as rallies follow declines, periods of high volatility grow out of quiet periods. The market is breathing, and Kerry tries to catch the point where it stops exhaling and starts inhaling.

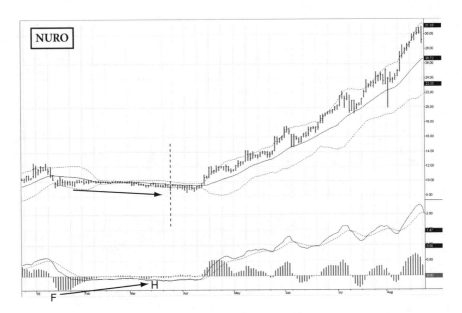

Figure 6.79A

Kerry calls this type of trade "a squeeze play." Shorting would not have been a good idea at the right edge of Figure 6.79, in view of a bullish divergence, F-H. Nor would have been buying—the stock continued to decline for several weeks, and most likely would have hit the stops on any long positions. The best entry was to place an open buy order near the upper edge of the recent range, to be stopped into a trade when volatility soared.

Answer 80

(Thanks to Bill Doane, for suggesting this question.)

A, B, C, and D. *Bonus:* A kangaroo tail.

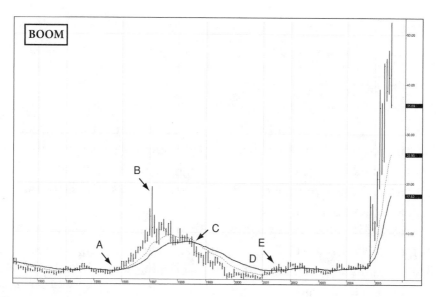

Figure 6.80A

"The larger the foundation, the taller the building," said Bill. After languishing below $4 for four years, BOOM, a member of the Industrial Metals group, exploded, rallying above $50 in less than a year, with very few pullbacks. Bill's concept—buying upside breakouts from multiyear bases—has brought home the bacon. Looking at point F, we can see that all statements were correct, except for E—it would not have been a good idea to short a stock that had already fallen to $2. Being ready to buy the upside breakout is, of course, essential.

The pattern in area B was a kangaroo tail—a one-bar stab to the upside from a congestion zone, showing that prices tested and rejected a higher level; this meant that the next move was likely to be down. The pattern at the right edge of the chart looks suspiciously like a precursor to another kangaroo tail. We won't know for sure until the next month, but you can suspect a tall bar stabbing to a new high and closing at the lows of being a part of a developing reversal pattern.

Answer 81

(Thanks to David Weis for suggesting this question.)

   1—C. 2—D. 3—A. 4—E. 5—B.

For a bar to confirm a rally, it has to exceed the high of the previous bar, and close higher, near the top, preferably on higher volume. An unconfirmed rally reaches a higher high than the previous bar, but does so on falling volume or fails to close near the high. Such unconfirmed rallies often lead to downward reversals.

This chart reflects 30 trading days in e-minis in July and early August of 2005, but its lessons apply to any market and any timeframe. Bar A was a kangaroo tail (with the low established on the day of the London Underground bombings). Notice that day's climactic volume, the highest for 30 trading days. A confirmed decline takes out the previous bar's low and closes lower, preferably on heavier volume than that of the previous day. An unconfirmed decline reaches a new low, but closes well off the lows or its volume shrinks.

Answer 82

(Thanks to Mike McMahon who provided his actual trade for this question.)

   Weekly chart (Figure 6.82-1): 1—A and B; 2—C-D; 3—D.
   Daily chart (Figure 6.82-2): 1—M-N; 2—P; 3—Q-R; 4—N; 5—Short.

The key question at the right edge of any chart is whether to go long, short, or stand aside. At the right edge of CAG on the day Mike decided to trade you could legitimately expect all three scenarios.

A bull could say that the EMAs were rising in both timeframes, with daily prices starting to reach the value zone, nearing a buy signal. A bear could say that a false upside breakout on the weeklies, coupled with a bearish divergence on the dailies, gave a shorting signal. Finally, you could say that with these contradictory signals you wanted to stand aside.

A successful trader knows what he is looking for and protects his trade with good money management. Mike's main focus at the time of this trade was shorting false upside breakouts and buying false downside breakouts. He saw what he needed on the weekly chart, got a confirmation from the bearish divergence on the daily chart, and put on his trade.

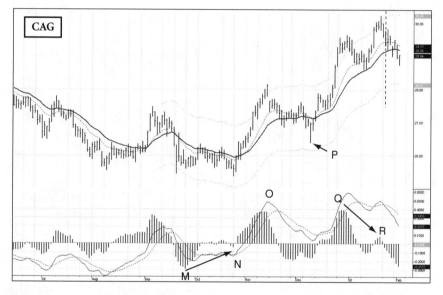

Figure 6.82A

Mike shorted Conagra on 1/26 and covered six trading days later after the stock plunged below its EMA on the daily chart. There it appeared to have staged a one-day reversal, poking down but then closing at the high of the day. Mike sent me excellent notes on this trade, reinforcing my respect for the clarity and integrity of his approach.

Answer 83

(Thanks to Kerry Lovvorn on whose actual trade this question is based.)

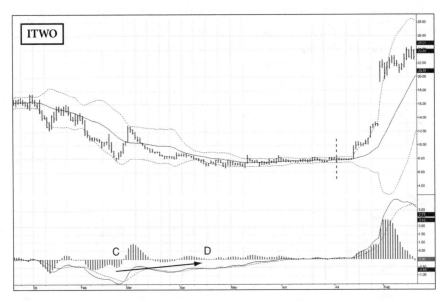

Figure 6.83A

1—A-B and D-E. 2—B-D. 3—C-D. 5 is correct.

Stocks and commodities go through periods of high and low volatility. Kerry watches for Bollinger bands to squeeze prices to identify periods of low volatility. He enters a trade when he expects volatility to jump. In an inexpensive stock, selling for under $10, buying is a more attractive option than shorting. Placing a buy stop above the tight range helps catch a surge in volatility.

Answer 84

(Thanks to Michael Brenke on whose actual trade this question is based.)

A—Up. B—Decreasing. C—Three. D—Short.

The slope of the moving average identifies an uptrend. The narrowing Bollinger bands identify declining volatility. MACD-Histogram, Momentum, and Stochastic all show bearish divergences.

Six days earlier, BBY rose to a new high in a low-range move with no follow-through. Shrinking Bollinger bands showed that the mass of traders did not participate in the upmove. There were bearish divergences in all indicators—MACD-Histogram and MACD-Lines, Momentum, and Stochastic. The inertia, identified by the EMA, was still up, but a bearish divergence of MACD-Histogram permitted it to override its bullish message.

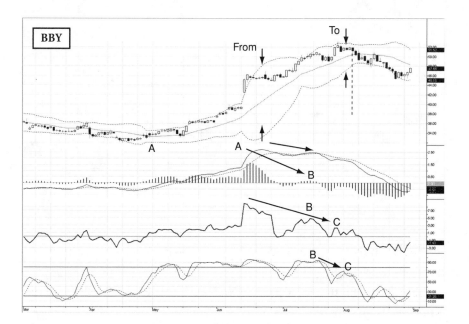

Figure 6.84A

Prices fell soon after the entry. The deepening bottom of MACD, the lowest in months, called for lower prices ahead. Finally, after hugging the lower band for over a week, prices began to stabilize; Stochastic and Momentum became oversold. The bearish signals had played themselves out, and it was the time to cover shorts.

Answer 85

(Thanks to Damir Makhmudov on whose actual trade this question is based.)

Figure 6.85A

Weekly chart (Figure 6.85-1): 1—E. 2—B. 3—Undervalued. 4—Short or stand aside.

Daily chart (Figure 6.85-2): 1—N. 2—M and O. 3—M. 4—Correct. 5 and 6—Incorrect.

A moving average identifies the mass consensus of value, and prices can normally get only so far away from it. When this distance becomes large, it shows that either bulls or bears are becoming stronger, and when it shortens, it means that they are becoming weaker and the trend might be ready to reverse. At the right edge of the weekly chart, prices are already below value, and bears are strong—F is deeper below value than D. Both EMAs and MACD-Histogram are declining—the Impulse system is in a full bearish mode.

At the time of Damir's entry into this trade, the daily EMA was declining but MACD-Histogram was rising, making the daily Impulse blue—neutral. There was no conflict with the weekly Impulse—with the weekly down and the daily neutral, it was okay to sell short. There would have been a conflict only if the weekly had been bearish while the daily was bullish, or vice versa.

Damir must have had a few tense days early in this trade when the daily continued to get stronger after he shorted. Being a discretionary trader and using a preponderance of evidence, he held his shorts; a strict system trader would have been stopped out when the daily Impulse turned green and stayed green for several days. The perfect time to enter the short side would have been in area P, where MACD-Histogram turned down and in gear with the weekly. Of course, such points are easy to see in retrospect, while traders like Damir have to make decisions at the foggy right edge of the chart.

Answer 86

Group 1: A, D, E, F, and J. Group 2: B, C, G, H, and I. *Bonus:* Just prior to D.

When Quest Diagnostics collapsed in summer 2002, the downturn of its 26-week EMA confirmed the downtrend (A). The stock stabbed down towards $25 repeatedly in 2002 and 2003. When it began to rally, the EMA ticked up (D), confirming the uptrend. No indicator is perfect, and in 2003 the EMA delivered a whipsaw, first ticking down (E), then up again (F). The new uptrend lasted for well over a year, until the summer of 2005, when the EMA turned down (J), marking the end of the bull market.

Moving averages represent a consensus of value, and well-established trends usually develop a certain rhythm. Prices keep pulling away from value in the direction of the trend, then snap back to the EMA, as if pulled by a rubber band. The downtrend in 2002 was punctuated by two rallies back to value (B and C). The uptrend in 2004 and 2005 was punctuated by three pullbacks to value (G, H, and I). Such signals occur in all timeframes, on daily and intraday as well as on weekly charts.

One of the most bullish things a stock can do is break down to a new low, show no follow-through to the downside, then rally and close above the previous swing's low. That's exactly what this stock did in the spring of 2003, before embarking on a healthy upmove that saw it more than double before the sell signal came in.

Answer 87

(Thanks to Andrea Perolo on whose trade this question is based.)

Weekly chart (Figure 6.87-1): 1—A and B; 2—E, F, and I; 3—C-D; 4—G-H.
Daily chart (Figure 6.87-2): 1—P-Q; 2—M-N; 3—N-O; 4—R.
Decision—Short.

The rise of the euro in 2003 paused in areas A and B. Later, in 2004, when the euro was declining from D to E, and in 2005, when it was declining from H to I, it found support at that same level. A zone of resistance on the way up became a zone of support on the way down. Notice how MACD-Histogram rallied at top G but was unable to rise above the zero line at top H. This "missing right shoulder" provided an especially strong warning of a coming reversal.

The daily chart shows an accelerating downmove. New downtrend-lines can be drawn to track prices, falling at a sharper and sharper angle. Near the right edge of the daily chart, the euro starts groping for a foothold. It traces a bullish divergence and breaks trendlines #3 and #2. Andrea writes, "the MACD during the last low shows that bears are simply missing"—it is another "missing right shoulder" reversal. He adds, "Curiously enough, the euro has a strong seasonal tendency to begin a strong rally around mid-July until mid-October."

Figure 6.87A

Going long worked out well for Andrea, as the euro rallied to the channel line, which he drew parallel to the new uptrendline. The new high of MACD-Histogram confirmed the strength of the rally. The decline from that initial peak found support at a higher level, but the latest rise is proving a little ragged; a weak MACD-Histogram makes you question the health of the uptrend.

Answer 88

(Thanks to Gerald Appel for suggesting this question.)

1—A and B. 2—A-B and E-F. 3—C through D. 4—B and F.
5—Long.

The one-month cycle in the NASDAQ, mentioned above, continued to
work during this trade—up one month, down the next. The market
was overvalued above the upper channel line and undervalued below
the lower line. It was approaching a buy zone near the right edge of
the entry chart, and is approaching a sell zone at the right edge of the
follow-up chart.

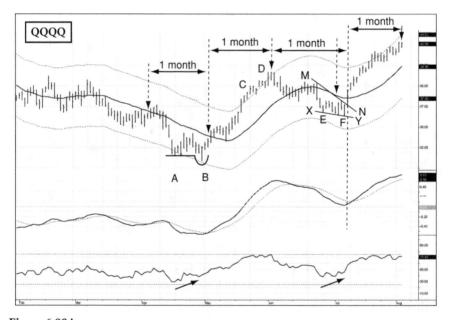

Figure 6.88A

At the right edge of the entry chart, a falling wedge, a potential false downside breakout, the bullish divergence of the RSI, and the one-month cycle combined to produce a strong buy signal. QQQQs rallied to the upper channel line and remained overbought for several weeks.

For a bonus point: When prices break to a new low at the right edge of the chart, you may suspect a true or false break, but you won't know for sure until some time has passed and you find out whether that break was confirmed or just a fake-out. An actual price break is something that occurred in the past and was confirmed by subsequent price action. An observer can afford to wait, but a trader must make his decision at the right edge of the chart, in the atmosphere of uncertainty.

Answer 89

(Thanks to Peter Tatarnikov on whose data this question is based.)

1—Down. 2—Down. 3—Down. 4—Buying. *Bonus:* Buy on breaking above the high of the previous bar.

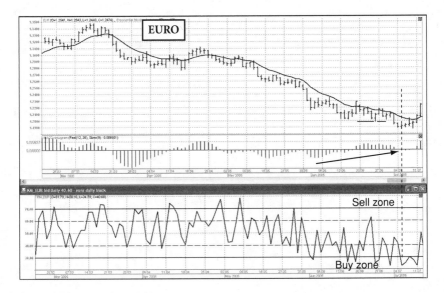

Figure 6.89A

The longer the trend, the greater the inertia of the market crowd. At the right edge of the entry chart, all indicators are down, although a very shallow low of MACD-Histogram shows that bears are losing strength. A 23% bullish reading means there are three bears for every bull. Since the total size of bullish and bearish positions is equal in the Forex market, an average long holds a position three times larger than an average short. With the crowd on the bearish side, the big traders must be on the bullish side. An extreme reading of bearish consensus suggests that an upside reversal is imminent.

A trend often goes on for a longer time and carries further than most people expect. Trying to catch a reversal is a risky business. To increase the margin of safety, it is better to enter positions not at the market but after prices begin to reverse. If bullish, place a buy order at the high of the latest price bar.

Answer 90

B, C, and E. *Bonus:* A kangaroo tail.

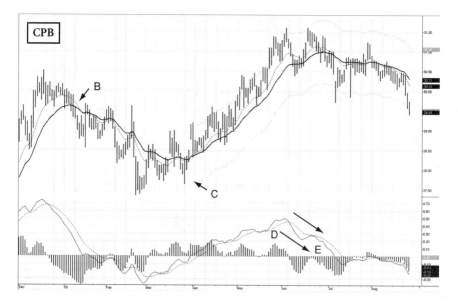

Figure 6.90A

I call this type of MACD-Histogram bearish divergence "a missing right shoulder." Prices rose to an equal height at tops D and E, but compare the height of MACD-Histogram peaks. At D, bulls were as strong as they have ever been during the preceding months. At E, they were nonexistent—unable to lift this indicator above zero. A simultaneous divergence of MACD-Lines reinforced this bearish message.

A channel trader takes profits on long positions near the upper channel line and on short positions near the lower line. The kangaroo tail near point C showed the last desperate push by bears—the market rejected lower prices and was ready to swing up, towards what became the D-E top.

Answer 91

(Thanks to Bill Doane for suggesting this question.)

C, D, and E. *Bonus:* False downside breakout.

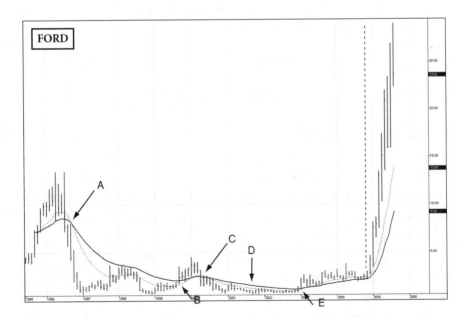

Figure 6.91A

One could make a bullish or bearish case at the right edge of the entry chart. Whenever you catch yourself squinting at a chart, stop immediately. Important trading signals leap from the charts—you cannot miss them.

The most prominent feature of FORD is its long base: After falling from over $13 to under $1, the stock remained flat for seven years. There is little point in trying to build a bullish or a bearish case for a stock that may remain in the cellar for many more years; it is important to realize that if and when it breaks out, it may fly. Sure enough, after closing above $4 and triggering a buy order, the stock rose to $29, making a new high every single month!

The pattern in area D is a false downside breakout. FORD fell below the support level that had held in 1996, 1998, and 2001. Then, instead of continuing lower and disappearing, the stock turned up, leaving behind the low water mark of a false downside breakout. At the right edge of the updated chart, one may feel tempted to start looking for a top, but the EMAs are still rising, identifying a bull market. It is important to use protective stops on long positions—it would be a shame to hold on a drop below the low 20s.

Answer 92

(Thanks to David Weis on whose concepts this question is based.)

1—E. 2—A. 3—C. 4—B. 5—D.

This chart reflects 29 trading days in cocoa in 2005, but its lessons apply to any market and any timeframe. A healthy rally is confirmed by volume; it shows that the rally is likely to continue. When prices rise but volume falls below that of the previous day, the rally is suspect.

An overnight gap occurs after the market gets hit by some overnight news, leaving a break between the high of one bar and the low of another. Trading in the direction of the gap means trading with the trend. A common belief is that gaps get filled, but that can take years.

In a confirmed decline a bar reaches a new low and closes near that low on increasing volume. Notice the power of the downmove in the middle of the chart—one confirmed down-day after another, with a couple of downside gaps thrown in for good measure. When prices fall but the volume declines, it shows that bears are becoming weaker.

Answer 93

(Thanks to Diane Buffalin on whose trade this question is based.)

True: 1, 2, 3, and 5. *Bonus:* Kangaroo tail.

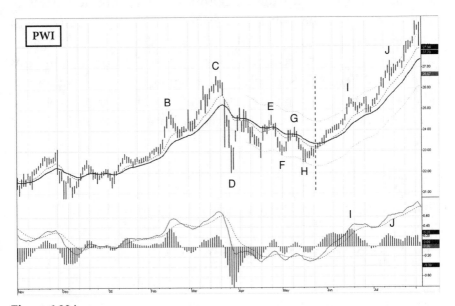

Figure 6.93A

In analyzing stocks one rarely sees a clear message flashing on the screen. It is much more common to put together several pieces of evidence and decide whether the bullish or the bearish case carries a greater weight. It helps to use a combination of weekly and daily charts, but in the example sent by Diane she used only the daily. At the time of her entry into the trade the downtrend was running out of time. The bears stabbed down and recoiled at point D, made three more attempts to push prices down, but could never keep them below 23. The combination of this support level, the false downside breakout below F at H, and a bullish divergence (D-F-H) builds up the bullish case.

When you are bearish, you can sell a call and keep the premium if the stock declines. When you are bullish, you can sell a put and keep the premium if the stock rallies. Both are intelligent alternatives to shorting or buying the actual stock. Since options are wasting assets, the time works for you when you sell them; the time works against option buyers. Diane traded the stock because of low option premiums at the time of her trade; she exited at the right edge of the chart, at the end of a day during which the stock fell on its widest range in months. Had I been long, I would have sold this stock after a bearish divergence (I-J).

Answer 94

(Thanks to Gerald Appel for suggesting this question.)

1—A, B, and C. 2—B-C. 3—D, E, F, and G. 4—G-H. *Bonus:* Short.

When the stock market blows out of its channel, it becomes severely overbought or oversold, depending on the direction of the breakout. Even during strong trends, such breakouts are usually followed by pullbacks into the channel. A bullish divergence (B-C) of the RSI at the time when the market was below its channel preceded a major upside reversal. A bearish divergence (G-H) when the market was above the channel preceded a major downside reversal. In this example, RSI rather than MACD divergences helped nail important reversals.

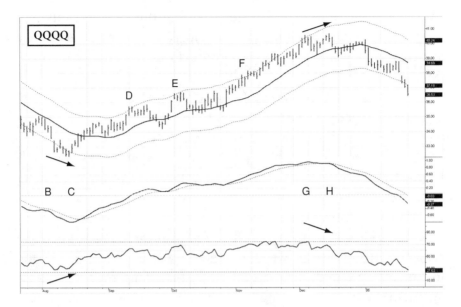

Figure 6.94A

Gerald Appel almost always puts envelopes around his moving averages, allowing him to know at a glance when the market is overbought or oversold. He adds a few indicators, looks for divergences, and uses their combinations with channels to identify tradeable reversal areas.

Grading Your Answers

If a question requires only one answer, you earn a point by answering it correctly. If a question requires several answers (for example, "Which two of the following five statements are correct?"), rate your answer proportionately. If you find both answers, give yourself a point, but if only one, then half a point.

You do not have to earn a perfect score in this section—different traders focus on different methods. Still, it is a good idea to familiarize yourself with the methods of your competitors. Forewarned is forearmed!

42–50: Excellent. You have not wasted your time reading *Entries & Exits*. You have grasped the methods of most traders interviewed in it—and now you can choose the ones you liked best and focus on those.

34–41: Fairly good. You have picked up the essence of the methods of some traders in *Entries & Exits*—but not enough of them. Look up the answers to the questions you've missed, review them, and retake the test in a few days.

Below 34—Poor. Markets are harsh and unforgiving, and only a small minority performs well enough to trade for a living. Missing more than a third of the answers on this test is a dangerous sign. Please pay attention to this warning bell. Go back, review the techniques described in *Entries & Exits*, and then retake this test.

TRADERS SPEAK

Answer 95

Correct—A, C, and D.

Time, patience, and reflection are hugely important factors. Success tends to lead to more success, and failure breeds more failure; a person who lost in one market is likely to lose in another. Planning is essential—even a day-trader should have a clear idea what markets he is going to watch and what patterns he is going to trade.

Answer 96

C, D, and E.

You want to trade with the crowd during trends and against it at turning points. Always going against the crowd is a poor idea. Long-term successful trading involves little emotion. It is better to develop methods that win on balance and apply them consistently, without worrying too much about any single trade. Women as a group tend to be more successful than men because their trading is less ego-driven and more profit-oriented.

Answer 97

Correct—A, C, and D.

Overtrading is one of the leading causes of traders' mortality. When in doubt, reduce the amount at risk—when less certain, trade a smaller size. Doubling up on a losing position usually means throwing good money after bad. The only exception to this occurs when you build a large position in several preplanned steps and the first portion shows a small loss.

Answer 98

Correct—B, C, and D.

A key advantage of a private trader over an institutional employee is his ability to stand aside until he sees the setup he wants. Amazingly, most people throw away this advantage, out of an itch to do something. Having a trading plan, made when the market was closed, is a key defense against impulsive trading. People who wait for the fundamental news tend to lag behind those who act on their chart signals.

Answer 99

A and E.

Moping over missed opportunities is as useless as gloating over successes—a mature trader works on perfecting his method, without becoming emotionally caught up in every single trade. The best time to cut and run from a losing position is immediately after it turns against you. The first loss is the best loss. The longer you wait, the more you lose; most traders sell out in fear and disgust just as the stock gets ready to reverse. The best thing to do is to run fast; failing that, reduce your position and hold.

It is perfectly okay to discuss your closed positions with trusted friends, but not to talk about open trades. Finding yourself in a losing trade sends a signal that you are wrong on that market; occasionally it makes sense to reverse a position, but as a rule it is best to stand aside and reevaluate that market from the sidelines. The market does not know how much profit you're trying to take—you have to take what it gives you and leave when the trend starts running out of steam.

Answer 100

Correct—A, B, D, and E.

There are as many ways to lose money as there are traders, but they boil down to following your opinion instead of paying attention to market reality. All successful traders have learned to put external limits on every trade, regardless of their opinion or intuition.

Answer 101

A and D.

Follow your rules and do not deviate from them, no matter how tempting a trade may appear. Look for the setups you tested and learned to trust. The brand of trading software makes little difference, as long as it is a functioning toolbox. Keep in mind that there is much randomness in the markets—a good setup will occasionally lead to a loss, while a violation of your rules may bring in a profit. Such deviations disorient beginners, but professional traders continue to follow their rules, expecting to come out ahead in the long run.

Grading Your Answers

If a question requires only one answer, you earn a point for a correct answer but zero points for a wrong one. If a question requires several answers (for example, "Which three of the following five statements are correct?"), rate your answer proportionately. If you find all three, give yourself a point, if two, 0.66, and if only one, 0.33.

There can be nothing permissive about the grading of this section. These are direct questions based on the interviews you have read—you either were paying attention or you weren't.

6–7: Excellent. There are few things as pleasant as a journey with an attentive companion.

5: Fairly good. Please look up the answers to the questions you've missed, review them, and retake the test in a few days.

Below 5: Poor. The only consolation is that trading is a life-long pursuit. You have the time to reread *Entries & Exits* and come back later to earn a decent grade on this essential test.

A LIFETIME OF LEARNING AND PRACTICE

Trading is an old man's game—and now, increasingly, a woman's. There are few if any young geniuses in trading. Experience and practice confer tremendous advantages. Intellectually, trading is not anywhere near as demanding as teaching calculus, trying cases in court, or performing appendectomies. On the other hand, it places massive demands on your psychology, maturity, and judgment.

If practice and experience play a key role in your success, your first goal should be to survive long enough to learn. Once you learn to survive, the next goal is to grind out small, steady profits. After you have proven to yourself that you are a steady, competent trader, you can raise your eyes to the next great goal—trading for a living. That's when you can live anywhere in the world, be independent from the routine, and not answer to anybody.

Many amateurs put the cart far ahead of the horse and shoot for spectacular profits without taking care of their survival in the markets. I created these two books—*Entries & Exits* and this *Study Guide*—to help you survive and succeed on your road to trading for a living. I encourage you to practice, study, and retake these tests until you earn an excellent score in each of the seven sections: Organization, Psychology, Markets, Trading Tactics, Money Management and Record-Keeping, Case Studies, and Traders Speak.

Now that we have come to the end of our journey together, what is next?

By now I must have convinced you of the necessity of keeping good records. Go ahead and set them up if you haven't already done so. I also must have impressed on you the life-or-death importance of money management—go ahead and implement those rules. Making many small trades will help you learn. Develop a trading plan—and please feel free to use one of the systems in *Entries & Exists* as your starting point.

Halfway through creating this *Study Guide* I flew to a resort in Cyprus to run a Traders' Camp. One morning I came down for breakfast and stopped by the table of the two brothers who owned that charming resort. "I heard you wrote a book that can make me rich," said one of them. "Right," I answered. "There is also a book I'm going to buy: *How to Run a Resort*. After reading it I am going to open a resort across the road and compete with you." The brothers doubled up laughing. After they recovered, one of them said, "I am afraid there is much more to running a resort than what could fit in a book."

You could not walk for more than five minutes in that resort without running into one of the brothers. They were completely on top of every detail. They were successful, enjoyed life, collected antique cars, but man, did they work. I created this *Study Guide* to show you how to put your shoulder into the harness and start moving towards success. There is no easy way, but there is a way.

My main reward for creating this book will come if and when we meet in the future and I hear from you that it helped you steer the course towards winning and freedom. I wish you success.

Dr. Alexander Elder
www.elder.com
New York City
February 2006

ACKNOWLEDGMENTS

If my publisher loaded me with work by asking to create this *Study Guide*, several persons helped take some of it off my shoulders.

Martin Knapp flew to New York, read the manuscript of *Entries & Exits,* and helped generate most of the charts in this *Study Guide*. He also participated in several brainstorming sessions during which we discussed potential questions.

Kerry Lovvorn was the first person to work with this *Study Guide*. I sent the text and the charts to him in Alabama, and he took the time to take every test and critique several questions and answers.

Carol Keegan Kayne did what she does with every book I write—she went through my English with a fine-tooth comb and brought me into full compliance with her high standards. Inna Feldman, my manager, kept the office humming while I stayed away working on the book.

Many thanks to the traders interviewed in *Entries & Exits* for sending me additional trades which I used in creating this *Study Guide*. I look forward to seeing you again in the future and comparing notes on our trades.

Dr. Alexander Elder